HENGE MONUMENTS

OF THE

BRITISH ISLES

Jan Harding

TEMPUS

First published 2003

PUBLISHED IN THE UNITED KINGDOM BY:
Tempus Publishing Ltd
The Mill, Brimscombe Port
Stroud, Gloucestershire GL5 2QG

PUBLISHED IN THE UNITED STATES OF AMERICA BY:
Tempus Publishing Inc.
420 Wando Park Boulevard
Mount Pleasant, SC 29464

British Library Cataloguing in Publication Data.
A catalogue record for this book is available from the British Library.

ISBN 0 7524 2508 0

Typesetting and origination by Tempus Publishing.
Printed in Great Britain by Midway Colour Print, Wiltshire.

CONTENTS

Introduction   6

1   Social transformation and the first henge monuments   7

2   Architectures of meaning   35

3   Experiencing henge monuments   59

4   Henge monuments, ceremony and society   83

5   The end of henge monuments   107

Bibliography   122

Index   126

INTRODUCTION

The monuments of the third millennium BC offer some of the most unmistakable and widely recognised images of British archaeology. A celebrated example is Stonehenge, its magnificent stone settings visited by many and used extensively to promote Britain's tourist industry (**colour plate 1**). Today's visitors are often disappointed by what they see, commenting that the site is smaller than they expected. But they are the unlucky majority who are kept away from the stones. For those fortunate enough to cross the roped boundary, and wander freely amongst the megaliths, there is little doubt that Stonehenge deserves its international accolade. Then there is Avebury, barely some 20 miles to the north, a site whose overwhelming size impresses the many who pass through the imposing earthworks (**colour plate 2**). Its bank and ditch contain a large part of the modern village and would have originally enclosed as many as 247 large standing stones. It is difficult not to be dazzled by cultural achievement on such a scale.

Both Stonehenge and Avebury are examples of a type of site which was commonplace in many parts of Britain between 3000-2000 BC. These are collectively described as henge monuments, a term first coined in the 1930s (Kendrick 1932, 83-98). Over 120 are now known, found from Cornwall to Orkney, and most have in common a circular, or more often than not, asymmetrically shaped or oval ditch, an outer bank, either one or two opposing entrances, and an external diameter of between 66ft-820ft (20-250m). These shared features define what one account has described as the 'classic' henge (Harding & Lee 1987, 30), but there is also significant variation in the design of these sites. Differences occur in their size and have led to the identification of sub-types or categories. There are the so-called 'mini-henges', which usually range from 16ft-46ft (5-14m) in their overall size, whilst at the other end of the spectrum are the giant 'henge enclosures' – of which Avebury is one example – with diameters of between 1050-1761ft (320-537m). Variation also exists in what lies within the earthworks. Some contain nothing but open ground, but others, like Stonehenge and Avebury, enclose standing stones, timber uprights or pits.

If henges are a physically distinctive and often spectacular class of monument, their purpose is nevertheless enigmatic. Originally described as 'meeting places' or 'temples', this interpretation has gained little over the years, in part because relatively few sites have been excavated, or at least excavated on a sufficiently large scale. But the current evidence hints at a story which is both intricate and fascinating. It highlights the ways in which henges may have been used by 'real people in real worlds' (Pitts 2000, 29) – their specific roles or meanings, and those more general social processes and developments with which they were so closely connected. This is a complex story of profound change, of new religious movements, of cultural invention, themes which are bound into this book's structure. I will focus on henge origins (chapter 1), their design and the implications for understanding later Neolithic religion (chapter 2), the activities undertaken within and around the monuments (chapter 3), their wider socio-political significance (chapter 4), and finally, why people stopped building these 'meeting places' or 'temples' (chapter 5). I am greatly indebted to Benjamin Johnson for the book's illustrations.

1

SOCIAL TRANSFORMATION AND THE FIRST HENGE MONUMENTS

There was no sudden outburst in the building of these assembly-places. Nor was it uniformly spread. Radiocarbon assays from early henges show this.

Burl (2000, 32)

Out of this period of social change arose a tradition of monument building which had its roots in the past but is most plausibly to be viewed as a method of integrating different parts of an embryonic society in a single undertaking.

Wainwright (1989, 30)

Henge monuments and the later Neolithic

The advent of the Neolithic in the British Isles, at around 4000 BC, represents a profound break from the previous hunter-gatherer way of life. The beginning of the period is marked by the introduction of horticulture, the keeping of domestic livestock, and new material technologies including pottery and ground stone tools. It was also early in the fourth millennium BC that the first monuments were built and it is for these that the Neolithic is best known. Thousands of impressive funerary and ceremonial sites can still be seen today and their importance is difficult to over estimate. They were the first attempt to quite literally 'alter the earth', and as such, stand as the most visible and tantalising statement of the beliefs and values of Neolithic communities.

The British Neolithic spans both the fourth and third millennium BC. Over such a long time-span there would have been a great deal of change and the period can be divided into at least two major phases. The communities of

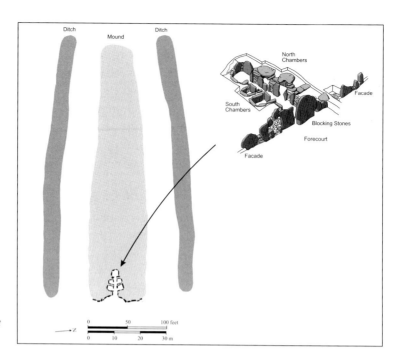

1 *The early Neolithic burial monument of West Kennet, Wiltshire*

2 *The early Neolithic causewayed enclosure of Windmill Hill, Wiltshire.* After Whittle *et al.* 1999, fig. 227

3 *Grooved Ware pottery of the later Neolithic*

the *early* Neolithic (4000-3000 BC) can be described as small and largely egalitarian, leading a mobile lifestyle and exploiting both domesticated and wild resources. Their impressive long barrows and megalithic chambered tombs (**1**), most of which contained 'collective' burial deposits, illustrate local ancestor worship, and many communities were also part of larger social alliances, meeting seasonally at huge open earthworks known as causewayed enclosures (**2**). However, the widespread abandonment of these monuments, along with the appearance of new types of material culture in the first few centuries of the third millennium BC, suggest dramatic social change and is taken as the beginning of the *later* Neolithic (3000-2200 BC). These innovations include highly decorated bucket-, barrel- or bowl-shaped vessels called Grooved Ware (**3**), a range of elaborate and presumably prestigious stone and flint objects, and the first henge monuments, with their inner ditch, outer bank and one or two entrances (**4**). Together these changes are seen to indicate the replacement of earlier lifestyles by new religious beliefs and practices, a more sedentary existence and increased social centralisation.

It is the henge monuments, more than the other developments, which symbolise the later Neolithic. These distinctive circular earthworks – which sometimes contained internal settings of pits, posts or stones – are the archetypal ritual sites of the third millennium BC. They are not only the most numerous and widely distributed of all Neolithic monuments, with over 120 definite and probable examples known from across the length and breath of the British Isles, but often assumed enormous proportions, especially on the chalklands of Wiltshire and Dorset where four sites had external diameters of over a thousand feet (**5**). It is evident, in other words, that large amounts of time and labour would have been expended on their construction and this has been explained in two ways. Some regard them as connected to a new and powerful set of religious beliefs and practices, even with a specialised priesthood whose authority was based on their supernatural and astronomical expertise. Alternatively, they are the product of a centralised form of political leadership, or chiefly élite, whose power was dependent on mobilising sufficient labour for such large-scale communal endeavours. Either way, the henge monuments are seen as a 'hallmark of their age' (Harding & Lee 1987, 66).

Both explanations infer that the first henges represent a transition to a different, and perhaps more complex, form of society. They also suppose that the monuments continued to be constructed throughout the later Neolithic, presuming these new beliefs or forms of socio-political authority were stable during this period. But are these assumptions perhaps too simple? As explanations they certainly pay scant regard to the *constitution* of the later Neolithic transition, assuming that the period merely 'appears' as something new and distinctive on the eve of the third millennium. This fails to explain why the transformation occurred in the first place or the role of henge monuments. Moreover, there is no detailed examination as to whether the onset of this

4 *The 'classic' henge of Arbor Low, Derbyshire.* Crown copyright: NMR Riley Collection

period was actually so instantaneous – akin to a 'revolution' sweeping across the British Isles – or more chronologically protracted, perhaps illustrating a gradual process of change. As the quotations at the beginning of this chapter suggest, these questions can only be resolved by considering the available chronological evidence for the earliest henges, to see if these sites suddenly appeared as a distinctive type of monument at the very beginning of the later Neolithic. It is equally important to consider whether the earliest examples were typical of the chronologically later henges, or was this a tradition of construction which changed through time, indicating both discontinuity and variation in the fabric of later Neolithic society?

The earliest henge monuments

The chronology of henge monuments is poorly understood. There are now over 100 available radiocarbon determinations, yet only 32 of these actually date initial henge construction. Most of the others are from contexts which either pre- or post-date the building of the bank and ditch earthwork, and it is often unknown whether they did so by a few centuries or just a few years. The remaining dates are from inner features whose chronological relationship with the rest of the site is not always clear, although many are likely to have been connected to the primary use of the monument. The limitations

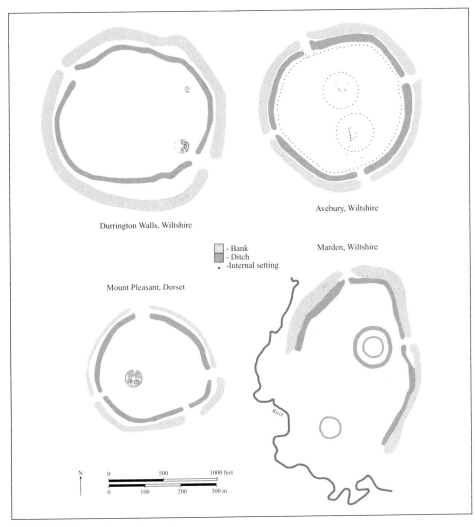

5 *The 'henge enclosures' of the Wessex chalkland*

with the dating evidence are exasperated by a series of plateaux in the cali-brated radiocarbon chronology of the late fourth and first half of the third millennium BC, which makes the dating of single events very problematic and masks the chronological dynamic of much of the later Neolithic. In short, any activity which originally occurred between 3100-2900, 2850-2650 and 2600-2480 BC will always yield dates of around 4400, 4200 and 4000 BP respectively (BP, or 'Before Present' with the present taken as AD 1950, refers to 'radiocarbon years' prior to conversion into 'real' calendar years, or BC). The result is a flattened chronology for much of the third millennium BC – not at all helpful when it comes to accurately dating the development of these monuments.

Despite these limitations it is possible to offer some basic thoughts on the chronological origin of henges. The available radiocarbon dates from primary contexts illustrate a long currency of construction and use, extending from the last few centuries of the fourth millennium to the early second millennium (**6** & **table 1**). But importantly, there does appear to be a distinction in the layout of sites built most likely *before* and *after* 2800 BC. The earliest dated monuments include the first phase of Stonehenge in Wiltshire, known hereafter as Stonehenge I, and the henges of Coneybury, also in Wiltshire, Llandegai A in Gwynedd, the Stones of Stenness in Orkney, Balfarg Riding School in Fife and Dorchester Site 2 in Oxfordshire (Avebury, despite a single date suggesting the contrary, is unlikely to be so early). But of these, both Stonehenge I and Llandegai A can be considered as *atypical* henges in that they each have an internal rather than more normal external bank (**7a** & **7b**); the site of Balfarg Riding School is unusual since it does not appear to possess an entrance or bank (**7c**); and the exceptionally small site of Dorchester Site 2 has also produced no evidence for a bank of any kind (**7d**). Therefore, of the six dated sites which may belong to the end of the fourth millennium, and the first two centuries of the third millennium, it is only the Stones of Stenness – with its internal ditch, outer bank and single entrance (**7e**) – which definitely has *classic* henge-like architectural features, although aerial photographs of Coneybury have revealed what is probably the remains of a bank (**7f**). By contrast, all sites dated to after 2800 BC possess an outer bank, inner ditch and at least one entrance, although one possible exception is Whitton Hill 1, Northumberland, a 'mini-henge' with four narrow causeways and no trace of a bank (Miket 1985, 137-44).

This may suggest that 'classic' henges – or circular earthworks with a bank, internal ditch and usually one or two entrances – were actually only one part of a more complex process of development. The Stones of Stenness being the only definite 'classic' henge likely to have been built before 2800 BC is of interest given that Orkney has often been seen as a possible point of origin for these enclosures. This remarkable single-entrance monument, with its inner stone circle (**colour plate 3**), has produced a single date of 3100-2650 BC from its primary ditch fill, and is located a short distance from another 'classic' henge, the Ring of Brodgar (Ritchie 1975-6). Its full significance, however, is only apparent when we consider other contemporary developments. Excavations at a number of the henge monuments located across the chalklands of Wiltshire and Dorset have produced large quantities of Grooved Ware pottery, and this has led some to consider both monument and pottery as closely linked phenomena, even as components of a single socio-religious complex of artefacts, practices and beliefs. The earliest known Grooved Ware is actually from Orkney, dating to no later than 3000 BC, and so it is assumed that this ceramic tradition, and hence the associated henge monuments, originated here and subsequently spread together across the British Isles. This may be a tenuous assumption, lacking any direct evidence, but would certainly account for the early date of the Stenness 'classic' henge.

But how do you account for the other early henges and their atypical characteristics – sites subsequently referred to as *formative* henges. Were they actually part of the same tradition of construction, regardless of whether it originated in Orkney or not, or the product of independent developments? To address these questions we can turn to the chalklands of southern England, a region which has produced a relatively well-dated sequence of monuments belonging to the late fourth and early third millennium BC. I have already referred to the atypical characteristics of Stonehenge I, built around 3000 BC on the eastern Salisbury Plain. As has been recently argued by Ros Cleal (1995a), the unhenge-like arrangement of its perfectly circular perimeter, with an internal rather than external bank, is paralleled by the segmentary nature of its ditch, the existence of at least two but probably three entrances, and the intentionally placed deposits in some of the ditch terminals of ox jaws and a skull. These characteristics all hark back to an older tradition of monument – best typified by the causewayed enclosures of the early Neolithic – suggesting 'that early Stonehenge owed more to the traditions of the preceding centuries than to a new and innovative "henge" tradition' (Cleal 1995a, 113). Indeed, such deliberate acts of retrospection are emphasised by some of the ox bone found in its ditch already being ancient when deposited.

This implies that the 'classic' henge was preceded by a transitional or 'formative' type of circular enclosure – an even greater probability when we consider the recently excavated Flagstones Enclosure (Healy 1997), located on the outskirts of the modern town of Dorchester in southern Dorset. No one has suggested that this site should be classified as a henge, particularly since it was probably built between about 3300-3000 BC. But it does possess an interesting fusion of architectural features. As with Stonehenge I, the segmentary appearance of its ditch is reminiscent of the layout of causewayed enclosures, and the site appears to be without an outer bank (**8**). Similarly, the interrupted ditch produced the articulated and disarticulated remains of two child burials, deposits which are well represented at a number of causewayed enclosures. Yet despite all these comparable features, the perfectly circular shape of Flagstones clearly anticipates a form of design we would expect more of henges than the typically oval or D-shaped early Neolithic enclosures, and Cleal (1995a, 114) has concluded that the monument is 'overwhelmingly similar' to the early enclosure at Stonehenge.

When taken together, then, the two sites suggest continuity between the late fourth and early third millennium BC. Other contemporary developments add to this picture. Round barrows, or circular mounds of earth covering small numbers of human burials, in either an articulated or disarticulated state (**9**), are known to have been constructed in some regions between the early fourth and the beginning of the third millennium BC.

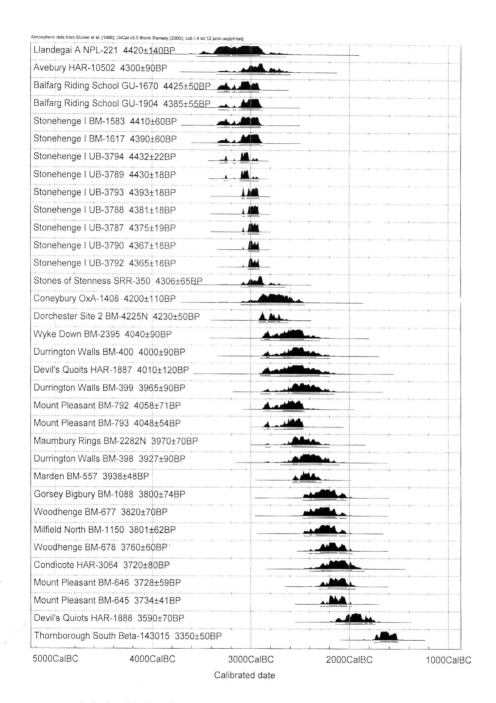

Atmospheric data from Stuiver et al. (1998); OxCal v3.5 Bronk Ramsey (2000); cub r:4 sd:12 prob usp[chron]

Llandegai A NPL-221 4420±140BP

Avebury HAR-10502 4300±90BP

Balfarg Riding School GU-1670 4425±50BP

Balfarg Riding School GU-1904 4385±55BP

Stonehenge I BM-1583 4410±60BP

Stonehenge I BM-1617 4390±60BP

Stonehenge I UB-3794 4432±22BP

Stonehenge I UB-3789 4430±18BP

Stonehenge I UB-3793 4393±18BP

Stonehenge I UB-3788 4381±18BP

Stonehenge I UB-3787 4375±19BP

Stonehenge I UB-3790 4367±18BP

Stonehenge I UB-3792 4365±18BP

Stones of Stenness SRR-350 4306±65BP

Coneybury OxA-1408 4200±110BP

Dorchester Site 2 BM-4225N 4230±50BP

Wyke Down BM-2395 4040±90BP

Durrington Walls BM-400 4000±90BP

Devil's Quoits HAR-1887 4010±120BP

Durrington Walls BM-399 3965±90BP

Mount Pleasant BM-792 4058±71BP

Mount Pleasant BM-793 4048±54BP

Maumbury Rings BM-2282N 3970±70BP

Durrington Walls BM-398 3927±90BP

Marden BM-557 3938±48BP

Gorsey Bigbury BM-1088 3800±74BP

Woodhenge BM-677 3820±70BP

Milfield North BM-1150 3801±62BP

Woodhenge BM-678 3760±60BP

Condicote HAR-3064 3720±80BP

Mount Pleasant BM-646 3728±59BP

Mount Pleasant BM-645 3734±41BP

Devil's Quoits HAR-1888 3590±70BP

Thornborough South Beta-143015 3350±50BP

5000CalBC   4000CalBC   3000CalBC   2000CalBC   1000CalBC

Calibrated date

6 *Radiocarbon dates from primary henge contexts.* Courtesy of Kevin Brown

Site	Date cal BC Sigma 1 (68%)	Date Cal BC Sigma 2 (95%)
Llandegai Site A (NPL-221)	3340-2910	3550-2650
Avebury (HAR-10502)	3090-2700	3350-2600
Balfarg Riding School (GU-1670)	3270-2920	3340-2910
Balfarg Riding School (GU-1904)	3090-2910	3330-2880
Stonehenge I (BM-1583)	3270-2910	3340-2900
Stonehenge I (BM-1617)	3100-2910	3330-2880
Stonehenge I (UB-3794)	3260-3020	3310-2920
Stonehenge I (UB-3789)	3100-3020	3270-2920
Stonehenge I (UB-3793)	3080-2920	3090-2910
Stonehenge I (UB-3788)	3020-2920	3080-2910
Stonehenge I (UB-3787)	3020-2920	3080-2910
Stonehenge I (UB-3790)	3020-2915	3030-2910
Stonehenge I (UB-3792)	3020-2915	3030-2910
Stones of Stenness (SRR-350)	3030-2870	3100-2650
Coneybury (OxA-1408)	2910-2600	3100-2450
Dorchester Site 2 (BM-4225N)	2910-2700	2920-2620
Wyke Down (BM-2395)	2860-2460	2900-2300
Durrington Walls (BM-400)	2840-2340	2900-2200
Devil's Quoits (HAR-1887)	2900-2300	2900-2200
Durrington Walls (BM-399)	2620-2300	2900-2150
Mount Pleasant (BM-792)	2850-2470	2880-2450
Mount Pleasant (BM-793)	2830-2470	2870-2460
Maumbury Rings (BM-2282N)	2580-2340	2850-2200
Durrington Walls (BM-398)	2570-2280	2700-2100
Marden (BM-557)	2560-2340	2580-2280
Gorsey Bigbury (BM-1088)	2400-2060	2470-2030
Woodhenge (BM-677)	2410-2140	2470-2030
Milfield North (BM-1150)	2400-2130	2460-2030
Woodhenge (BM-678)	2290-2030	2410-1970
Condicote (HAR-3064)	2280-1970	2400-1850
Mount Pleasant (BM-646)	2210-2030	2300-1940
Mount Pleasant (BM-645)	2200-2030	2290-1980
Devil's Quoits (HAR-1888)	2040-1770	2140-1740
Thornborough South (Beta-143015)	1690-1520	1750-1510

Table 1 *Radiocarbon dates from primary henge contexts should be interpreted as a chronological range based on its mean and standard deviation (see left-hand column of figure 6). The range is calculated to either 1 standard deviation on either side of the mean, when there is a 68 per cent chance of accuracy, or to 2 standard deviations, when there is a 95 per cent chance of accuracy.* Courtesy of Kevin Brown

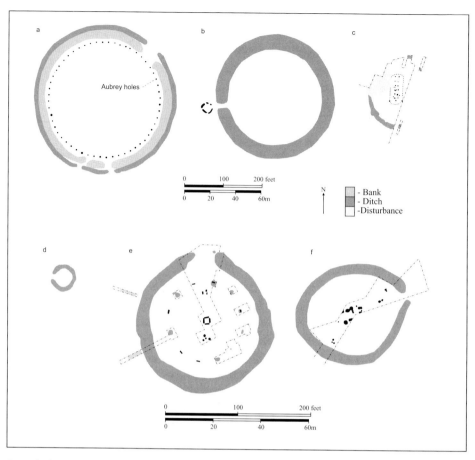

7 *Early henge monuments: a. Stonehenge I, Wiltshire (after Cleal 1995a, fig. 36) ; b. Llandegai A, Gwynedd (after Houlder 1968, fig. 1); c. Balfarg Riding School, Fife (after Barclay & Russell-White 1993, illus. 6); d. Dorchester Site 2, Oxfordshire (after Whittle et al. 1992, fig. 7); e. Stones of Stenness, Orkney (after Ritchie 1975-6, fig. 2); f. Coneybury Hill, Wiltshire (after Richards 1991, fig. 97)*

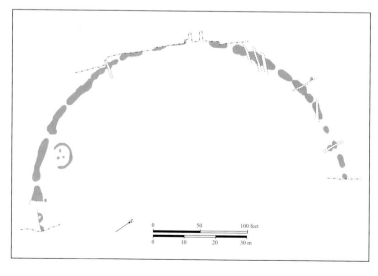

8 *The Neolithic enclosure of Flagstones, Dorset. After Healy 1997, fig. 18*

However, what little we know about their chronology suggests that it was not until about 3500 BC that the erection of these mounds was often accompanied by the digging-out of adjoining pits to form as many as three encircling ditches (**10**). That these enclosures were indeed a middle fourth millennium development is reiterated by a series of ring ditches, or what are usually interpreted as the remains of plough-razed round barrows, dated to between 3500-2900 BC (**11**). Hence, the digging-out of small circular enclosures, only broken by one to two entrances, was a tradition of construction which appeared in the latter half of the early Neolithic, and is broadly contemporary with a decline in the construction of causewayed enclosures. And this was a fluid or changing style of construction, for there is a tendency for the enclosures surrounding round barrows to become less segmentary and less irregular as the fourth millennium drew to a close. It is possible, in other words, that they produced at least some of the inspiration for the design of the later 'formative' henges.

Importance was thereby placed on digging out more or less continuously ditched perimeters during the later fourth millennium and these circular enclosures were associated with the burial of dead individuals. The continuity of this connection into the later Neolithic is demonstrated by two of the most impressive funerary monuments of this era – Duggleby Howe (Kinnes *et al.* 1983), in east Yorkshire, and Maes Howe (Renfrew 1979, 31-8; Richards 1992, 448), far to the north in Orkney. Both consist of a massive round mound set at the centre of incomplete but large enclosures with diameters of 1,200ft (370m) and 490ft (150m) at Duggleby and Maes Howe respectively (**12** & **13**). At Duggleby, inhumations and cremations had been placed in a deep central pit and throughout the covering mound, and whilst the spectacular stone-built passage and chambers at Maes Howe are thought to have been robbed of their human bone, they similarly played an important role in funerary practice. The chronological relationship between these mounds and their enclosures is yet to be ascertained, but radiocarbon dates at Maes Howe suggest that its ditch is likely to have been cut early in the third millennium. If a similar date is applicable to Duggleby's ditch, then what we may have are examples of a new tradition of circular enclosure very similar to the broadly contemporary, if much smaller, 'formative' henges of Stonehenge I, Balfarg Riding School and Llandegai A. In fact, the Maes Howe enclosure is strikingly reminiscent of the nearby 'classic' henge of Stenness. Excavations have demonstrated that the ditch was likewise very wide and, most importantly, possessed an external bank.

The connection between burial mounds and largely uninterrupted enclosures is also evident in Ireland. Here the later fourth millennium sees the development of the distinctive passage graves, their stone-built chambers acting as repositories for burnt and unburnt human bone. These often formed cemeteries, or groups of monuments, and it has recently been noted that the best preserved and most distinctive of these, located along the River Boyne in eastern Ireland, are also

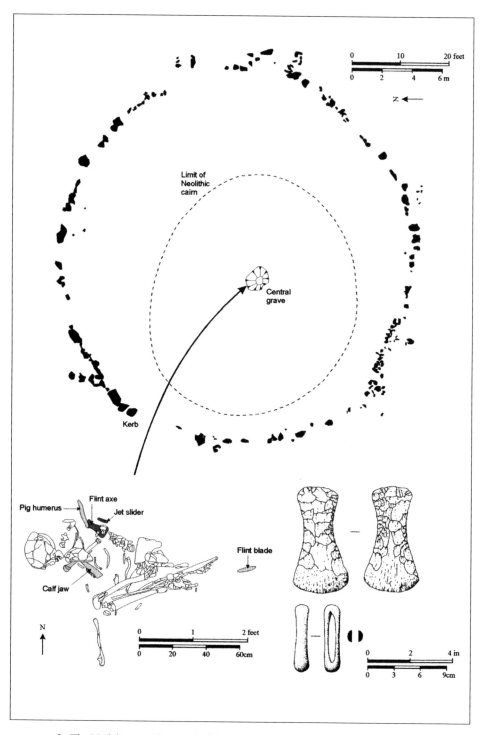

Limit of
Neolithic
cairn

Central
grave

Kerb

0   10   20 feet
0   2   4   6 m

Z ←

Pig humerus

Flint axe

Jet slider

Calf jaw

Flint blade

N

0   1   2 feet
0   20   40   60cm

0   2   4 in
0   3   6   9cm

9 *The Neolithic round barrow of Whitegrounds, East Yorkshire.* After Brewster 1984 associated with henge-like enclosures (Condit & Simpson 1998; Cooney 2000, 165-73). There are three such sites, each consisting of an impressive circular bank but no accompanying ditch, one of which, like Maes Howe, encircled an earlier passage grave. A similar relationship is evident at both Tara, Co. Meath, and Ballynahatty, Co. Down, where a ditched and banked enclosure respectively were built around a pre-existing passage grave. Whilst largely undated, these and other enclosures are thought to have been built early in the third millennium, and if so, suggest parallel developments on either side of the Irish Sea. The similarity with Maes Howe is of particular interest given that communities in Ireland and Orkney are often thought to have been in contact with one another.

It can be concluded that the 'formative' enclosures – which have a circular shape, are usually interrupted by one or more entrances, but atypically for henges, possess a segmentary ditch and commonly lack any outer bank – were part of a much more complex tradition. That they were not so much a new phenomenon, as the reworking of an existing heritage of practices and material resources, would certainly account for why all three dated 'formative' sites were in some way connected to the dead. The enclosure at Balfarg Riding School surrounded an earlier timber structure interpreted as a raised platform upon which human corpses were placed (Barclay & Russell-White 1993). This had been burnt down and buried under a round mound prior to the digging out of the ditch. Excavations at Llandegai A found a single cremation under its

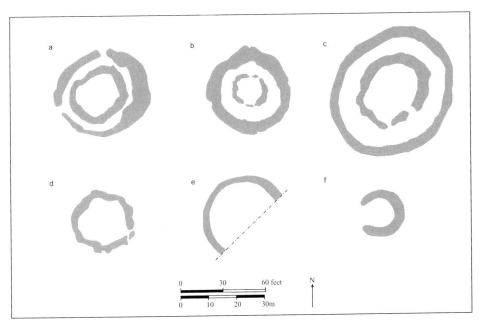

10 *The ditch layouts of Neolithic round barrows: a. Grindale 1, East Yorkshire; b. Boynton 3, East Yorkshire; c. Aldwincle 1, Northamptonshire; d. Handley 27, Dorset; e. Holborough, Kent; f. Handley 26, Dorset*

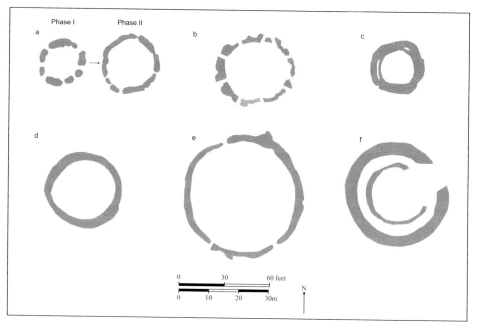

11 *Excavated ring ditches: a. Dorchester II, Oxfordshire; b. Dorchester I, Oxfordshire; c. Firtree Farm, Dorset; d. City Farm 4, Oxfordshire; e. Litton Cheney 1, Dorset; f. Newnham Murren, Oxfordshire*

bank, whilst immediately outside the entrance, in the ditch fills of a small segmentary sub-circular enclosure, were greater quantities of burnt bone (Houlder 1968). Similarly, the early enclosure at Stonehenge is associated with a large number of cremations in its so-called Aubrey Holes, a circular setting of 56 postholes along the circumference of the ditch. The Aubrey Holes date to the monument's first phase of construction, but at some point during the early or middle third millennium the posts were removed and cremations placed in their upper fills, as well as into the enclosure's ditch and bank. Mention should also be made of the small oval-shaped site of Sarn-y-Bryn-Caled Site 2, Powys, and the four cremations found in its ditch (Gibson 1994, 159-61). Radiocarbon dates from the recut of the enclosure suggest its general contemporaneity with the other 'formative' henges.

But this still leaves a crucial question – what is the relationship between these 'formative' enclosures and the 'classic' henges? Did they evolve into the later sites or did the henge tradition proper have an independent origin, perhaps in Orkney as so often assumed? Unfortunately, the present evidence fails to provide a definitive answer to this important question, but the chalklands of southern Wessex offer some interesting hints. Let us start by considering the eastern Salisbury Plain (**14**). The architectural repertoire of Stonehenge I, with its irregular but more or less continuous earthwork perimeter, was reworked at a subsequent building event on Coneybury Hill located less than a mile away. Here a regularly excavated ditch, broken by a single entrance and most likely associated with an outer bank, was established around a pre-existing arrangement of pits in the first half of the third millennium BC (Richards 1990). The site can certainly be described as a 'classic' henge and its development may be contemporary with the deliberate backfilling of part of the earlier enclosure at Stonehenge. This new tradition of monument was then to flourish from about 2600 BC with the construction of two adjacent sites: the truly massive henge at Durrington Walls (**5**) was an imposing enclosure more than 1,640ft (500m) across, containing two large timber structures (Wainwright & Longworth 1971); and nearby, the very much smaller Woodhenge, which also contained concentric timber settings (**24**). The sequence of construction across this wind-swept chalkland could therefore indicate that 'classic' henges emerged out of, and then replaced, the earlier tradition of monumental enclosure at Stonehenge. At the same time, the early date of the Coneybury henge makes it less likely that Orkney, far to the north, was the only point of origin for this new tradition of monument.

A similar sequence is evident with the impressive monuments clustered around the market town of Dorchester in south Dorset (**15**). But the chronology and pace of change is somewhat different, perhaps demonstrating the role of local factors in the adoption of the henge tradition. The enclosure of Flagstones had been out of use for some centuries before its segmentary design was in part replicated at Maumbury Rings (**16**), where a circle of an estimated forty-five near-vertical shafts, with an average depth of 34ft (10.4m), were dug into what may have been an original ditch at some point in the mid-third millennium BC (Bradley 1976). Despite its highly unusual appearance, the site also possessed the outer bank so characteristic of 'classic' henge monuments.

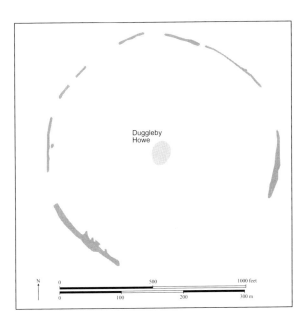

12 *Duggleby Howe, East Yorkshire.* After Kinnes *et al.* 1983, fig. 7

13 *Maes Howe, Orkney.* Crown copyright: RCAHMS, John Dewar

Indeed, like Coneybury, Durrington and Woodhenge, this most striking of earthworks demonstrates the increasing significance now attached to physically separating an enclosed space from the surrounding landscape – a trend which is reiterated by the massive Dorchester timber circle erected nearby a century or so earlier. Then, at some point in the mid-third millennium, an imposing monument akin to Durrington Walls was established at Mount Pleasant (**5**), employing architectural features clearly typical of 'classic' henge monuments. Its massive inner ditch and outer bank enclosed an area up to 1,214ft (370m) across, within which was a further henge monument, itself some 141ft (43m) in diameter (Wainwright 1979). Just like Woodhenge, this inner site contained concentric timber settings.

The evidence from these two landscapes suggests that 'classic' henges represent the crystallisation of existing local practices and architectural resources into a more clearly defined tradition of construction. Yet such a sweeping statement should be considered in light of its implications. For if these sites did indeed *evolve* across southern Wessex, then how do we account for the henges known elsewhere? Did the 'classic' henge originally develop across these chalklands and then spread to the rest of Britain, and if so, why were these remarkable monuments so widely adopted? And is such an explanation likely, given the early date already noted for Stenness in Orkney, far to the north? Alternatively, did the 'classic' henge independently evolve in *more than one region*, suggesting a number of complementary and essentially similar sequences? This implies remarkable cultural homogeneity, which would, in turn, require an explanation – put simply, what social processes could be responsible for these wide-ranging similarities?

Religion and the origin of henge monuments

The limitations with the present radiocarbon evidence make it difficult, if not impossible, to answer some of these questions. There are simply not enough good quality dates from their primary contexts to fix the geographical origin of the henge phenomenon. Hence, it may be more rewarding to focus on the social mechanisms behind their spread and explain why the monuments of the fourth millennium BC were so completely superseded by these enclosures. Of particular interest in this regard are the religions of this period, for henges are widely seen to have played a significant role in the spiritual life of later Neolithic communities. That they should be understood as ritual centres, as opposed to settlements, is borne out by the conformity in their design – a common feature of places of worship – and the lack of everyday rubbish from their ditches and interiors. But if the spread of henge monuments testifies to the increasing popularity of the religious beliefs and practices with which they are associated, what is the relationship between the 'world view' of *early* and *later* Neolithic communities? Were they largely similar or was a new religion introduced during the third millennium BC?

Everything we know about the early Neolithic suggests that communities were organised into small groups who placed considerable importance on their

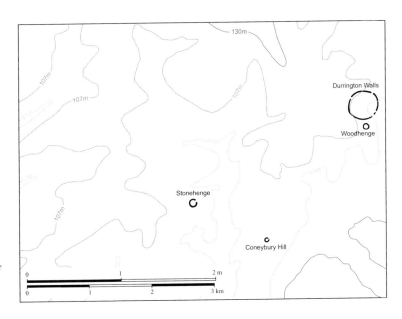

14 *The henge monuments of the eastern Salisbury Plain, Wiltshire*

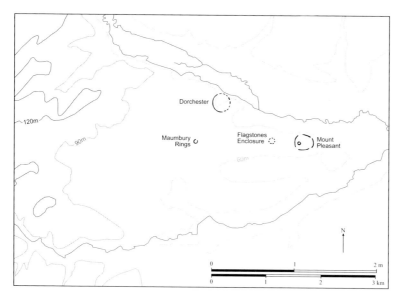

15 *The henge monuments of Dorchester, Dorset*

ancestry. They built and used their own burial monuments – the long barrows and megalithic chambered tombs – and it is within these that one finds the disarticulated human bone of up to fifty individuals (**17**). The character of these deposits suggests that prime concern was attached to transforming the human body from the fleshed state of the individual into a collection of bone, and this has been associated with beliefs centred on ancestor worship. In societies where similar practices are still performed, the fate of the living is seen to reside in their communal ancestral spirits. These ghosts are responsible for either the success or failure of the community, and for this reason 'sacrifices' or tribute are provided to appease the ancestors. It would be wrong to assume that such a system can be directly translated into the early Neolithic, but the giving of gifts to the spirit world would certainly account for some of the more unusual deposits found at the burial monuments and causewayed enclosures. These include complete cattle skeletons or neat bundles of cattle bone, deliberate arrangements of human bone, particularly skulls (**18**), and exotic items like polished stone axes or carved chalk objects.

But this early Neolithic religion of ancestor cults may have been threatened by new beliefs and practices. The round barrows, covering a few human burials in either an articulated or disarticulated state, have already been discussed. There appears to have been a decline in the number of individuals interred under these monuments and by the beginning of the later Neolithic they are usually associated with just one, two or three articulated burials, accompanied by a rich array of objects including finely made flint axes and knives, boar tusks, bone pins and jet belt-sliders. This gradual move towards the commemoration of specific individuals is matched in southern England by the development of short or oval long barrows, a type of monument known to have sealed a few

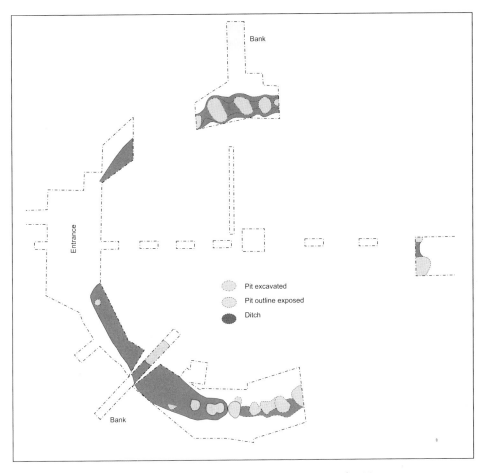

Bank

Entrance

Pit excavated
Pit outline exposed
Ditch

Bank

16 *Maumbury Rings, Dorset.* After Bradley 1976, fig. 13

articulated burials instead of larger amounts of disarticulated bone, accompanied in one instance by a polished flint knife, arrowhead and jet belt-slider (**19**). The few dated examples belong to either the close of the fourth millennium or the first few centuries of the third millennium. All this evidence may indicate that the traditional system of communal ancestry was being complemented, if not partially replaced, by one whereby specific individuals were glorified after their death – suggesting perhaps that some ancestors, and maybe their descent groups, had become more important than others.

That traditional religious authority was in decline is illustrated by other evidence from the end of the fourth millennium BC. There is a noticeable drop off in the construction of more established forms of burial monument – although an impressive range of chambered tombs, including Maes Howe, may have first appeared in north Wales and parts of northern and western Scotland – and the only two long barrows known to have been built after 3000 BC, possibly dating to very early in the third millennium, both possess oval mounds. A turning away from older customs may be emphasised by some of the megalithic burial monuments from across the Cotswold-Severn region, where access to the burial chambers seems to have been deliberately blocked by either the filling in of the chamber and passage or the adding of stonework to their entrances. This admittedly undated phenomenon suggests the importance attached to taking places of ancestral worship out of service. A changing social picture is also illustrated by the fact that no new causewayed enclosures were built after about 3300 BC and that they had been completely abandoned by the close of the millennium. Nowhere is the end of this tradition more striking than at Crickley Hill, Gloucestershire, and Carn Brae, Cornwall. Large numbers of arrowheads suggest that both were attacked and these acts of violence could be responsible for the demise of each enclosure.

Social change and a faltering religion may be central to understanding the henge phenomenon. The earliest 'formative' enclosures were part and parcel of this gradually transforming and perhaps unstable 'world order', their appearance and deposited remains combining tradition with innovation and novelty. But the development of 'classic' henges, with their more continuous ditches and external banks, represents a radical break with the past, an attempt to create new places of religious worship, places which were associated with a distinctive set of beliefs and practices. In this sense, their emergence is akin to a religious 'revolution' and this would certainly account for their rapid adoption in some parts of the British Isles, as illustrated by the broadly contemporary radiocarbon dates from Stenness and Coneybury, the two earliest known 'classic' henges sited nearly 500 miles apart. There are certainly parallels from

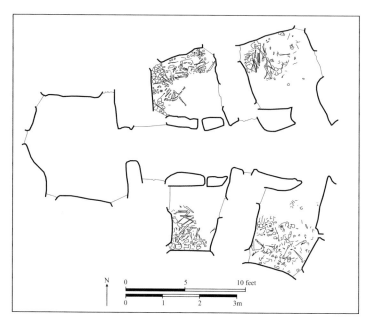

17 *The human bone deposits at the early Neolithic burial monument of West Kennet, Wiltshire*

18 *A skull deposited at the early Neolithic causewayed enclosure of Hambledon Hill, Dorset.* Copyright courtesy of Roger Mercer

history. New religious movements − such as the spread of the 'ghost dance' among the Plains Indians whose land and livelihood had been devastated by the arrival of Europeans, or over a more extended timescale, the spread of Christianity across parts of the Roman Empire − often became quickly popular over large distances because they were seen to offer salvation, spiritual renewal and the ability to resist, or escape from, social upheaval and oppression. It is tempting to consider the henges, and all they represent, as offering solutions to the problems and uncertainties encountered by people early in the third millennium BC.

A break with the past is not only evident in the distinctive design of 'classic' henges. In all likelihood the beliefs with which they were associated were no longer based on localised notions of ancestry. Although human bone was deposited, many of the excavated sites are without them, and when they do occur it is usually in small quantities (see below). The only exception is where the bone has been cremated, a practice already noted in relation to the 'formative' henges of Stonehenge I and Llandegai A. The majority of the evidence is from four so-called 'mini-henges' at the Dorchester on Thames complex in Oxfordshire (Atkinson *et al.* 1951; Whittle *et al.* 1992), each associated with large numbers of cremations placed across their interiors, in the upper ditch fills and immediately outside the outer lip of their ditches (**20**). The only dated site is Dorchester Site 2, belonging to the early third millennium, but its similarities with the others suggest their broad contemporaneity. The likelihood of an early date is illustrated by perimeters of conjoined oval pits resembling Stonehenge I and Flagstones. If correct, this would suggest that cremation became intrinsically linked to the new circular enclosures of the early third millennium. However, these remains are not generally found on the 'classic' henges, suggesting that the incorporation of human bone, whether burnt or unburnt, had become far less common by the middle of the third millennium, as illustrated at Dorchester, where the impressive double-ditched Big Rings produced no such remains (Whittle *et al.* 1992, 184-93). The exception is the relatively early site of Wyke Down, in Dorset, dating to 2860-2460 BC (**21**). The similarities between the site's appearance and the Dorchester 'mini-henges' are very apparent and the upper fills of three of its pits contained a cremation, a human skull fragment and a compact mass of ashy soil with minute quantities of cremated bone (Bradley *et al.* 1991, 96, fig. 3.22).

It is therefore unlikely that ancestral beliefs were central to the roles and meanings of these sites, as it was with early Neolithic monuments, and perhaps the most obvious explanation is that the supernatural spirits now worshipped were no longer the relations, whether real or fictional, of local families or kin

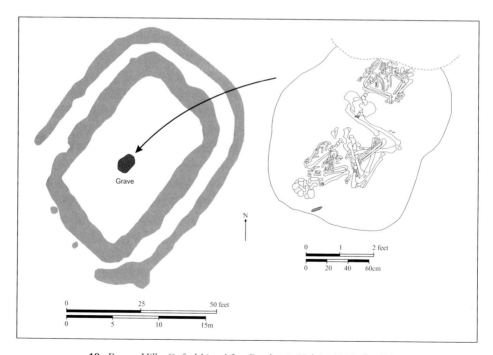

19 *Barrow Hills, Oxfordshire.* After Barclay & Halpin 1999, fig. 3.2-3

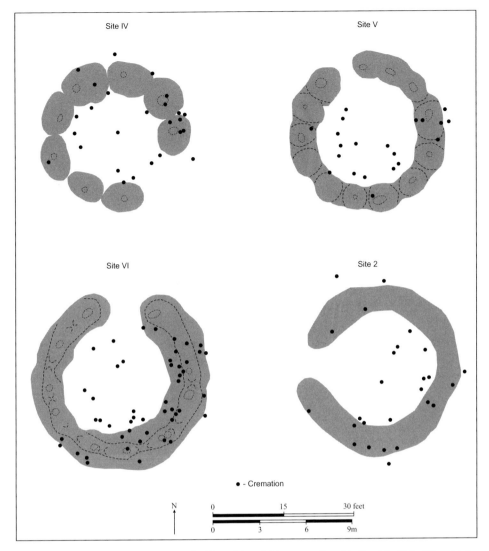

Site IV

Site V

Site VI

Site 2

● - Cremation

N

0   15   30 feet

0   3   6   9m

20 *The 'mini-henges' at Dorchester, Oxfordshire.* After Atkinson *et al.* 1951, figs 16, 19 & 22; Whittle *et al.* 1992, fig. 7

groups, but were rather connected to other phenomena. If so, this may represent a momentous transformation in religion. As Aubrey Burl (1987, 82) puts it, 'The power of ancestors seemed to have failed and their cult gave way to the worship of gods'. This may account for why many 'classic' henges are located away from fourth millennium monuments. In the Wessex chalkland, for example, their construction may have led to the creation of new ritual foci in areas where there were no physical traces of the old beliefs. This is certainly the case across the eastern Salisbury Plain. Whilst the first 'classic' henge, built on Coneybury Hill, was close to both long barrows and the early monument at Stonehenge, it was separated from them by a steep-sided dry valley. The other henges, sited close to the River Avon, are also spatially removed from these places of worship. Similarly, both Maumbury Rings and Mount Pleasant were built away from earlier foci. These two landscapes hint at discontinuity – as though the new supernatural order was seeking out places unpolluted by old ancestral ties. Elsewhere the henges are known to have been even more distant from older monuments, as in the upper Thames Valley, where they are usually over 2.5 miles (4km) from established monument complexes. The only exception is at Dorchester on Thames, where its remarkable series of henges, including Big Rings, was built alongside and inside a pre-existing long recti-linear enclosure known as a cursus. Here the norm may have been deliberately reversed in an attempt to make this a 'special' landscape, a conclusion certainly supported by the size and complexity of the Big Rings henge (see chapter 4).

But the introduction of henge monuments, and the possible conversion to a new religion, is likely to have been a complex process. As mentioned, their adoption in widely distant regions appears rapid when considered in terms of radiocarbon chronology, yet this is not to say that people's lifestyles changed overnight. The date of the first henge monuments could have greatly varied from area to area, suggesting that change did not occur simultaneously across the length and breadth of the British Isles. This is evident in the upper Thames Valley (22), where the earliest known 'classic' henge is that of the Devil's Quoits in Oxfordshire, probably dating to between about 2900-2200 BC (Barclay *et al.* 1995, table 6, 45), broadly contemporary with their introduc-tion across the Wessex chalkland. However, only 9 miles (15km) away are two other henge monuments, both of which may be significantly later than the

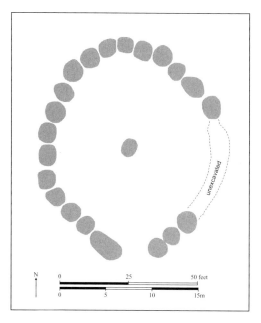

21 *Wyke Down, Dorset.* After Bradley *et al.* 1991, fig. 3.18

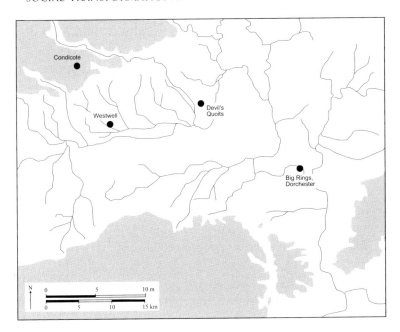

22 *The henge monuments of the Upper Thames Valley*

Devil's Quoits. On the edge of the Cotswolds, in the county of Gloucestershire, is the double-ditched site of Condicote, most likely belonging to either the last few centuries of the third millennium or the first few of the second millennium (Saville 1983). Further downstream from the Devil's Quoits is Big Rings, a site already mentioned. There are no radiocarbon dates from this monument, but its primary ditch fill has produced Beaker sherds, a distinctive type of pottery dating from the late third millennium, and also found in an early context at Condicote. Hence, there was no uniform 'pulse' of social change but a more complex process of monument construction which extended over hundreds of years.

There is, then, the possibility that the new beliefs co-existed with vestiges of the old religion. If so, it would not be surprising if there was a fusion of these different ideologies. One example may be the continued presence of human bone at a number of henge monuments. Ancestor worship is a common feature of many different recorded societies throughout the world – even existing amongst today's 'world religions' of Christianity, Buddism, Hinduism and Islam – and it seems probable that despite the important trans-formations in belief during the later Neolithic some people continued to be concerned with their own descendants. Deposits of both articulated and disar-ticulated bone, particularly long bone and skull fragments, are known from a number of excavated henges. There are also instances of complete, or nearly complete, skeletons, including in the ditch fills of three of the giant Wessex 'henge enclosures': two infant burials were found at Mount Pleasant, there was part of a child's skeleton at Marden in Wiltshire, along with a young adult female deposited some time after the ditch had been dug, and at Avebury the so-called 'dwarf-burial', another adult female, this time of diminutive height. The deliberate deposition of these remains is reminiscent of the early Neolithic, particularly since a disproportionately high amount of the human skeletal evidence found in the enclosures of the fourth millennium BC was also of children. This does not necessarily imply any meaningful continuity over such a long time-span, but could suggest that at least one older tradition was being incorporated, or even subsumed, within the newer beliefs and practices. It is certainly feasible that local communities, when converting to the new supernatural order of the later Neolithic, did not just draw strength from its novelty and innovation, but found a role, and presumably assurance, from some of the old ways.

The process of religious change was therefore more complicated than the phrase 'revolution' suggests. The term may evoke its importance but fails to capture a sense of its heterogeneous character. A similar point is made by the relationship between henges and another new monumental tradition. Alex Gibson (1998) has recently argued that a number of these sites were built around a pre-existing and impressive timber circle. In some cases, such as Arminghall, Norfolk, and North Mains, Perth and Kinross, these earlier monuments date to either the close of the fourth or the early third millennium BC (**23**), suggesting they were broadly contemporary with the 'formative' tradition of circular enclosure noted above – a connection very much reiterated by the circular setting of fifty-six postholes, or Aubrey Holes, dug within

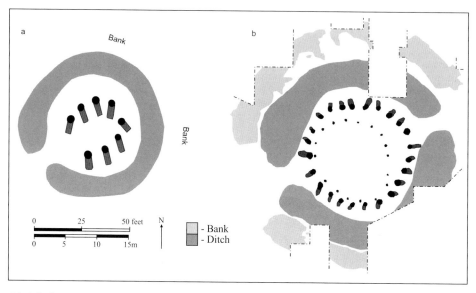

23 *The henge monuments of a. Arminghall, Norfolk (after Clark 1936, plate iv) and b. North Mains, Perth and Kinross (after Barclay 1983, fig. 3)*

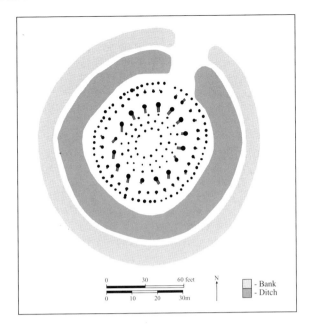

24 *Woodhenge, Wiltshire.* After Pollard 1995, fig. 2

the earlier enclosure at Stonehenge I. But the primacy of timber circles was to continue throughout the later Neolithic. It seems likely, for example, that the enclosures at Durrington Walls and Woodhenge, both dating towards the middle of the third millennium, may have similarly enclosed pre-existing, but very much larger and multi-circuit, rings of upright posts (**24**). Is it therefore possible that the earliest of these settings were symbols of the nascent religion, connected to the first acts of conversion as a place was adopted by the new religion? And does the association of complex timber circles with later henges suggest that in some areas they assumed an importance which was intrinsic to the function of these earthworks? This certainly seems likely on the Wessex chalkland where timber circles commonly occur within the henges.

Conclusion

Despite the all too apparent problems with the available radiocarbon evidence, it is possible to identify a number of key themes in the origin of henge monuments. A suitable starting point is not so much the beginning of the later Neolithic as the latter half of the fourth millennium BC. As already argued, this period witnessed the introduction of new architectural resources and practices – notably the digging out of circular and generally continuous ditches – which were to become increasingly popular in the first few centuries of the third millennium. But what followed, with the development of the 'classic' henges, was very much more than simply the end product of this sequence of social reproduction. The local process of translation which had been responsible for previous innovations in the use and layout of enclosures was itself disrupted by a more sweeping process of change, a tear in history which seriously distorted the strategies of social reproduction which had their origins in the later fourth millennium BC. The outcome was a new supernatural order whose currency would last for over 500 years.

It seems that in some regions of the British Isles the henges were part of what can be best described as a 'complex' or package of new practices and material culture, including both pork feasting and the use of Grooved Ware. Many of the excavated sites across the Wessex chalkland have produced large quantities of immature or young adult pig bone, generally regarded as the remains of feasting episodes. One can only speculate as to the extent to which this activity was connected to the new rituals and beliefs, particularly since cattle bone continues to occur at these henges. But the emphasis on pork, as opposed to the consumption of beef so prevalent at the earlier causewayed enclosures, suggests a shift in religious etiquette. A transformation was certainly evident at Stonehenge, where cattle remains dominated the faunal assemblage associated with the early 'formative' enclosure, but became far less common than pig during the currency of 'classic' henge construction. Grooved Ware pottery, which is thought to have spread from Orkney to the southern chalklands during the first few centuries of the third millennium BC, may have also played an important role in these feasts. These bucket- or barrel-shaped vessels (**3**), which often far exceed the size of other Neolithic pottery, were ideal for communal feasting and have been found in large quantities at many of the excavated henges in Wessex. That Grooved Ware was introduced as 'classic' henges spread throughout Britain is certainly suggestive, adding to the impression of radical, if protracted, social change.

This is not to say that the later Neolithic can be solely characterised by the onset of henges and new religious practices. Other innovations which date to this period include a diversification in the range of portable material culture and the appearance of what may be special purpose assemblages. These have been interpreted as part of a complex material language by which to 'segregate and distinguish between people, places and things' (Thomas 1996, 87), best illustrated by the development of a range of elaborate and presumably prestigious objects, including polished stone maceheads, carved stone balls, jet beltsliders, distinctive types of flint axes and a range of ornate pins. The beautiful craftsmanship of these 'special items' continues to appeal today, yet it is the henges, and all they represent, which provide the most distinctive legacy of the later Neolithic. It is these monuments, more than any other aspect of the archaeological record, which provide the most visible statement that the world inhabited by communities during the third millennium BC was very different to that which preceded it, and that which followed.

2

ARCHITECTURES
OF MEANING

The Neolithic world was not our world in a simpler form. To us it is a complex and elusive world, not because we cannot understand the farming methods or the carpentry techniques but because we cannot comprehend how the people themselves regarded those activities, what rituals were performed to make the wheat grow, what magical acts were needed before a house could be built.

Burl (1987, 80)

A henge was not just an earthwork, as it appears to us now. It was a significant locale, the location of particular activities, maybe too the location of specific occurrences or events in a belief system, for instance the place where epiphanies of gods were found, where contact with other worlds was to be had, or similar events.

Harding, A. (2000, 267)

Some light is thrown upon what went on in these sacred places by the plan of the monuments themselves.

Clark (1936, 25-6)

First principles

The opening quotation advises us to interpret people's beliefs during the later Neolithic – to understand the 'world view' or existential existence of those who inhabited the forested wildernesses and clearances of the British Isles during the third millennium BC. This is no simple task for all that is left of these beliefs are 'the discarded remnants and rubbish of the past, the objects lost and forgotten, with no inherent message, out of context, the feeblest specks of what once existed, sounds silent and gone forever' (Burl 2000, 64). Nevertheless, we must consider what these battered and incomplete remains tell us about how the world was seen. What do they say, if anything, about people's views as to the world's origins and why humans first walked the earth? Or how they understood the mysteries of birth and death? And do they provide any insights into their perception of human destiny or whether they believed themselves beholden to ancestors, spirits and gods? In the quest for the answers, the henge monuments are perhaps the most forthcoming later Neolithic evidence – for as the second quotation notes, they were places of public worship, arenas for enacting the religious beliefs and practices of the time.

Religious sites often conform to a stylised design which resonates with deeply symbolic meaning. Examples would include the oblong-shaped and colonnaded synagogues of Judaism, the cruciform churches of the Christian faith, and the minareted mosques of Islam. The architecture of each invokes emotions whose familiarity encourages compliance in both behaviour and belief on the part of the devotee. But how about 'classic' henges? Do they similarly possess shared physical features? And if so, what 'light is thrown upon what went on in these sacred places', to quote from the beginning of this chapter? At first glance, there indeed appear to be two basic concepts behind their design. The first is a circular, or near circular, shape. The origins of such a layout can be traced back to the early Neolithic, or so it was argued in the previous chapter, but by the beginning of the third millennium the circle had been widely adopted as the norm for ceremonial sites, in much the same way that the cruciform shape was to gradually become the standard for Christian centres of worship. The second concept is that of enclosure by way of a largely continuous ditch and earthen bank, a simple feature whose origins may again be found in the last few centuries of the fourth millennium, but which then mutated into a commonplace design whereby the bank was always outside the ditch.

These two elements were to have a largely unchanging appeal for a period of some 500 years. Consider the shape of those dated sites mentioned in the previous chapter. The 'formative' henges of Stonehenge I (Wiltshire) and Llandegai A (Gwynedd), the four early 'mini-henges' at Dorchester on Thames (Oxfordshire), and the possibly primordial 'classic' henge of Stenness (Orkney), all possess as close to a nearly perfectly circular external form as is possible given the practical realities of ditch-digging (**25**). The importance of a circular design was to continue throughout the third millennium (**26**), although a significant number of later enclosures possess a more asymmetrical or oval shape, as can be demonstrated by comparing the outlines of Woodhenge (Wiltshire), Devil's Quoits (Oxfordshire) and Wyke Down (Dorset) with the earlier monuments (**26a, b & e**). This almost pathological conventionality suggests that the circular shape was in some way central to the beliefs and practices which epitomised the new religious order of the later Neolithic, particularly since the earliest sites are the most perfect from this point of view – not at all surprising when we consider how the physical expression of any ideology is often most striking when first

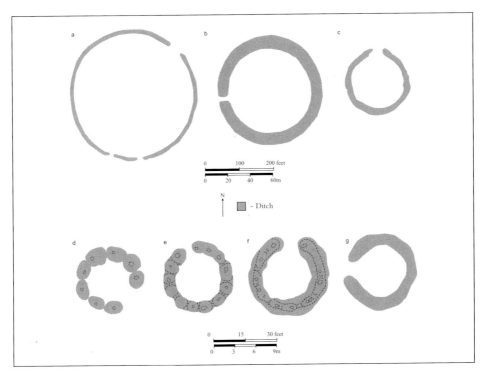

25 *Ditch layouts of 'formative' or early 'classic' henge monuments: a. Stonehenge I, Wiltshire; b. Llandegai A, Gwynedd; c. Stones of Stenness, Orkney; d. Dorchester Site IV, Oxfordshire; e. Dorchester Site V, Oxfordshire; f. Dorchester Site VI, Oxfordshire; g. Dorchester Site 2, Oxfordshire*

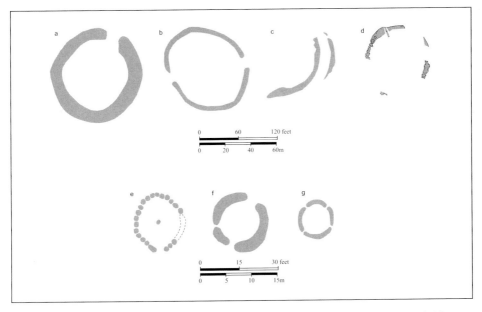

26 *Ditch layouts of selected henge monuments: a. Woodhenge, Wiltshire; b. Devil's Quoits, Oxfordshire; c. Condicote, Gloucestershire; d. Maumbury Rings, Dorset; e. Wyke Down, Dorset; f. Milfield North, Northumberland; g. Whitton Hill 1, Northumberland*

adopted. In fact, the only monuments which deviate significantly from the principle of circularity are the 'henge enclosures' of the Wessex chalkland: and variations in their shape could be connected to their massive size.

Conformity is also illustrated by the continuous henge perimeters. Their ditches and banks are interrupted by just one or two entrances, although a very small number of sites possess a third entrance, whilst two of the four 'henge enclosures' have four entrances, or in the case of Marden in Wiltshire, an unenclosed side facing a river. They therefore contrast with the causewayed enclosures of the early Neolithic – whose interrupted nature suggests open and fluid movement by those using the sites – and hint at the importance now placed on regulating access into and out of ceremonial centres. The significance of continuously enclosing space may also be illustrated by the emphasis placed increasingly during the third millennium on the digging-out of more regular ditches. The 'formative' henge of Stonehenge I consisted of a series of conjoined pits, a form of construction taken to extremes at the mid-third millennium 'mini-henge' of Wyke Down, where twenty-six chalk-cut pits were dug into a shallow connecting ditch (**21**), and at the broadly contemporary but very much larger site of Maumbury Rings, where an estimated forty-five near-vertical and extremely deep pits were cut into a connecting ditch (**16 & 27**). The 'classic' henge of Devil's Quoits, dating between 2900-2200 BC, also possessed a pit-dug ditch rather than a continuous trench. By contrast, many of the sites likely to date after 2500 BC (Woodhenge, Gorsey Bigbury, Condicote and the 'henge enclosure' of Durrington Walls) possessed less segmentary ditches, although the continuing importance of pit-digging is illustrated by the massive sites of Mount Pleasant and Avebury, their irregular ditches of intersecting pits interspersed with unexcavated spurs and ridges of natural chalk. The site of Milfield North, dating in all likelihood to the latter half of the third millennium, also possessed a segmentary form of construction, with low causeways separating ditch segments from one another.

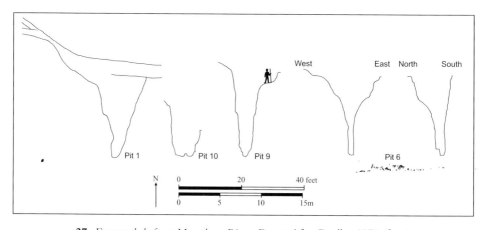

27 *Excavated shafts at Maumbury Rings, Dorset.* After Bradley 1976, fig. 4

Enclosing the cosmos

But what exactly does circularity and the more or less continuous enclosure of space tell us about the concepts, codes and customs which characterised the 'world view' of the later Neolithic? Perhaps the first thing to note is that henge monuments divide space into that which is 'inside' and that which is 'outside'. The act of enclosure creates a place which is different or separate from the excluded landscape, quite literally lifting sacred beliefs and practices out of everyday existence, and consequently protecting them from the corruption of the everyday or the challenge of mortals. It should also not be forgotten that sacredness is sometimes regarded as dangerous for any who come into contact with it unprepared (such as forgetting to take off one's shoes before setting foot on holy ground) and linked with sickness or even death. In this sense, the presence of the enclosing ditch and bank may have had the same effect as the walls which surround many centres of worship. Passing through these barriers reminds the visitor to adopt a respectful manner – to lower one's voice, to move slowly and quietly, to become acutely aware of their imperfections and mortality. For to act otherwise could very well be a risky business.

These perspectives help us understand why the henges had more or less continuous perimeters. Unlike the regularly interrupted banks and ditches of causewayed enclosures, their very design stressed the separation and containment of the enclosed sacred space – or what could have been conceived as 'purity' itself – from the surrounding landscape and its associated 'impurity'. This could even be why many henge earthworks are much more substantial than those surrounding earlier causewayed enclosures. A number of henge ditches survive to a depth of over 6ft (2m), and some are even deeper, such as up to 33ft (10m) at Avebury, and the truly remarkable shafts dug at Maumbury Rings, estimated to have been between 32.8ft (10m) and 36.8ft (11.2m) in depth. Earthwork widths are similarly impressive, with over half of all excavated ditches and banks being between 32-75ft (10-23m) and 32-118ft (10-36m) wide respectively (**28**). These barriers are very much in excess of what is practically required, surely emphasising to all who entered that they were now 'outside' of everyday existence: especially if, as we shall see in the following chapter, the banks largely blocked the view of the surrounding landscape. The importance of enclosing space also provides a context for the almost universal adoption of the circular, or near circular, shape, for this is the most compact two-dimensional figure available to design, thereby minimising the area of contact between the enclosed region of space and everything without. It is as though the monuments were conceived from the *inside out*. The priority for the builders was the inner sacred arena and the greater the interface with the outside world, the greater the risk of it becoming defiled or desecrated.

That they were planned from the inside out also makes sense of their rather striking perimeter layout. One of the distinctive characteristics of henges is that

28 *The central Thornborough henge, North Yorkshire.* Photography by Cambridge University Collection of Air Photographs

most invert the more usual earthwork sequence with the bank *outside* the ditch. This is certainly why these sites are so highly visible on aerial photographs. Such a layout makes little practical sense, unless it is, as Ian Hodder (1990, 264) has argued, to 'keep things in'. By this he did not mean humans or animals, but rather the dangerous and feared ideas, spirits or experiences associated with untamed nature. To Hodder the henges were a way of coping with this threat. If ramparts normally protect a site from the outside world, then their ditches and banks do the same, but in reverse. The insecurity of the outside world is now contained. As Hodder says, 'The "enemy" is now within', held captive by society itself, which is why, he claims, the earthworks are associated with the remains of wild animal species, a pattern clearly represented at a number of the excavated henge monuments on the Wessex chalkland. At Mount Pleasant, Durrington Walls and Woodhenge, the bones of wild boar and wild cattle were restricted to the outer ditches of the enclosures, in contrast to domesticated species, which were more common within the enclosures (Richards & Thomas 1984, 214). A similar wild/tame opposition was also evident at Maumbury Rings, albeit expressed in a rather different way. Here the animal bones excavated in the top 15ft (4.6m) of its remarkable shafts were dominated by the remains of red deer, yet these were very much in a minority lower down in their fills, where domesticated cattle and pigs dominated (Bradley & Thomas 1984). The available dating evidence suggests that these shafts filled rapidly and so the contrast was deliberate. It is also mirrored by human bone and pottery being restricted to the upper and lower parts respectively of the shafts.

One does not have to go along with Hodder's entire argument – and it is certainly simplistic to assume, as he does, that non-Western society distinguished between 'nature' and 'culture' – to accept that what was being enclosed by the henges was a symbolic representation of the outer world, or put another way, the world in microcosm. A similar perspective has been adopted in another recent discussion. Colin Richards (1996) suggests that henges reproduce the qualities of the surrounding landscape so that the finished site is a metaphor for the wider landscape. It was his investigations in Orkney which initiated the view. He noted how both the Stones of Stenness (**colour plate 3**) and the Ring of Brodgar (**colour plate 4**), two nearby henges located in a large natural basin on the Orcadian Mainland, reproduced the qualities of the surrounding landscape. Each is sited on the end of a narrow isthmus, surrounded on three sides by the lochs of Harray and Stenness, and beyond, by the hilly skyline (**29 & 30**). Richards considers this distinctive location as symbolised in the design of the henges. Their enclosing banks represent the surrounding hills – although there was only very slight evidence from Brodgar for the original existence of such a feature – and the lochs are mirrored by the rock-cut inner ditch of each

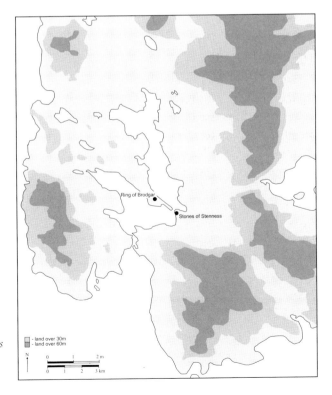

29 *The location of the two henges on the Mainland, Orkney.* After Richards 1996, fig. 5

☐ - land over 30m
■ - land over 60m

30 *An aerial view of the Ring of Brodgar, Orkney, and its surrounding landscape.* Copyright Richard Welsby

site, especially since they appear to have originally held water. It has even been claimed that the tall sandstone monoliths set within each of the monuments copied the height of the distant hills. He is suggesting, in other words, that the banks are the horizon, or physical rim of the builders' known world, therefore encapsulating or enclosing their social universe.

There is a close link between the two Orcadian henges and their surrounding landscape, and whilst Richards' arguments work less well for other monuments, it is nonetheless the case that some sites were built to deliberately reference prominent natural features. The substantial size of many henge banks restricts or funnels visibility through the site's entrances, and in hilly terrain, this could mean towards particularly impressive stretches of the horizon. Consider the cluster of henges strung out along the Milfield Basin, to the north of Northumberland (**31**). It has been argued by Anthony Harding (2000) that here there is a subtle interplay between the sites and the local topography. The view southwards through the entrance of the Coupland henge, for instance, is towards the foothills of the Cheviot massif, lying just a few miles away along one side of this natural basin. Similarly, the Milfield North henge frames to its south a number of distinctive summits, whilst a further henge, at Yeavering, is orientated eastwards towards a prominent local landmark and a line of distant hills (**32**). These sites reference the local topography, and the surrounding hills of the Cheviots, which were mirrored by the henge banks, are employed to enhance their monumentality. Prominent parts of the local landscape are thereby drawn into the inner world of the enclosures.

But why were the builders of henge monuments so concerned with symbolically representing their lived world? What did this metaphorical association mean to those who worshipped at the monuments? And what was its role within their religion? One way of addressing these questions is to consider the symbolic properties of the henge's circular design. The circle has historically been taken as a shape with either sacred or divine connotations. A few examples suffice to make the point. To many native North American Indians the circle 'stands for' the horizon, or the rim of the world, in a way which is very reminiscent of Richards' interpretation of henge monuments. This is not at all surprising if we consider that spherical vision – where the individual is at the centre of a world which recedes towards the horizon – is commonplace amongst people, such as the native North Americans, who inhabit open landscapes. The circle's edge is where the earth makes contact with the sky, where the two fuse together, creating life on the Great Plains across which these people roamed. Similarly, the Pueblo Indians of the Rio Grande depict the sun as concentric circles with a central cup mark, while the Yupik Eskimos of south-west Alaska picture the universe as a series of rings spreading out towards the horizon, where the cosmos was creased and earth becomes sky. There is also the medieval tradition of 'magic circles', where mystics drew circles within which they are protected from potentially hostile or evil forces: and a hint that this may have been just the most recent expression of an older tradition is provided by the Etruscan custom of ploughing an encircling protective furrow around an area where a city was planned.

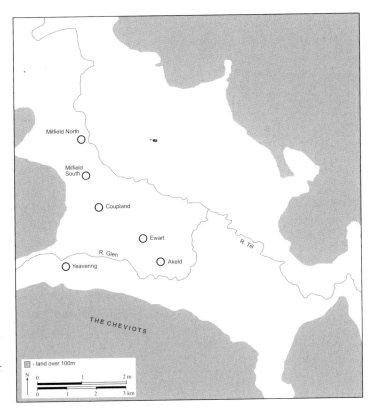

31 *The location of the Milfield Basin henges, Northumberland. After Waddington 1996, fig. 5*

32 *Looking eastwards through Yeavering, Northumberland, towards a small hill and the edge of the more distant Cheviots.* Copyright courtesy of Anthony Harding

Implicit to all these traditions, and many more beside, is the notion that the circle is no ordinary shape but possesses special qualities. It is commonly taken to represent cosmological wholeness and harmony, meanings whose inspiration were sometimes the very properties of the sun and the moon, celestial objects known to have permeated religious belief through the ages. They both embody circularity in their shape and cyclic motion through the sky, and as a result, are perhaps the ultimate symbol of continuity, renewal, predictability and perfection, or what one historian of religion eloquently describes as the 'eternal return'. The same can be said of the nightly circling of the stars. Hence, the use of circular space could evoke these very qualities and sensations, especially if the sun or moon were worshipped as deities or spirits, something which is common to many societies – for such a shape 'is "without a beginning and without an end" and as such is at once both a symbol of the cosmos and of the seasons and thus proof of the certainty of life beyond death' (Clare 1987, 470). All this provides a very useful interpretive framework. But the validity of these arguments must be considered in greater detail. It is necessary to enquire whether there is direct archaeological evidence for a circular, or near circular, design communicating or evoking these very properties during the later Neolithic. Can it be demonstrated, for example, that these monuments were indeed linked to celestial entities?

That henges may have had astronomical orientations has been most famously, and repeatedly, suggested for Stonehenge. Over the past 150 years it has been seen as a planetarium for skywatching, a solar temple, and an observatory for predicting the movements of the sun, the moon, and even the occurrences of eclipses. These are invariably complex arguments and usually depend on the alignment of some of its most prominent standing stones, of which the Heel Stone, set just outside the entrance to the monument, is the most notable. The fifty-six Aubrey Holes, which ring the inside edge of the bank, are also drawn into some of these convoluted arguments, dug, according to one writer, in positions which enabled the site to be used as a virtual computer for predicting eclipses. Yet the enthusiasm with which some of these claims have been made is misleading, for most can be disregarded on account of their uncritical use of the archaeological 'facts', their astronomical inaccuracy, and their misuse of statistics (Ruggles 1996; 1997; 1999, 136-8). What remains is the possibility that one of the three entrances at the 'formative' henge, built around 2900 BC, was orientated towards the northern limit of moonrise (**33a**); and more convincingly, that its later rebuilding in stone, commencing at around 2500 BC, was accompanied by a shift in the axis of its entrance to bring it into line with the rising midsummer sun (**33b & c**), its light 'pouring down a thin tunnel of stone' (Burl 1994, 91) and penetrating the closed confines of the monument's inner sanctum (**34**). But with such a complex site as Stonehenge, with its large number of timber and stone settings, even these alignments could have been fortuitous. Perhaps the only definite conclusion is that Stonehenge's layout 'did not incorporate precise astronomical alignments and did not function as an ancient "observatory" in any sense that would be meaningful to a modern astronomer' (Ruggles 1996, 15).

Do other henges demonstrate beyond any reasonable doubt the importance of celestial phenomena? Unfortunately, the evidence is again ambiguous, especially given the surprising lack of systematic research on this very subject. When compared to other types of Neolithic monument, such as stone circles or funerary sites, 'little is evident – or at least has been convincingly suggested – in the way of overt astronomical symbolism amongst these monuments' (Ruggles 1999, 131). There are, however, some tantalising glimpses in the immediate vicinity of Stonehenge itself. As we saw in the previous chapter, the earliest of the surrounding monuments was on Coneybury Hill, and its single entrance, like the later Stonehenge, was orientated to the north-east, towards the midsummer sunrise. Then there is Woodhenge with its six concentric rings of timber posts (**24**). The overall layout of these inner settings are elliptical and their major axes are again aligned to the north-east upon the summer solstice sunrise. Both sites therefore hint at the solar orientation of henges, and one author (Darvill 1997) has envisaged the entire Stonehenge landscape as a 'sacred geography', quartered according to the rising and setting of the sun at both the midsummer and midwinter solstices (**35**). He saw its eastern quadrant, which included the henges of Coneybury, Durrington Walls and Woodhenge, as associated with 'sunrise, new beginnings, life, light, fertility, feasting, water, and the earth', whilst the western quadrant was linked to 'sunset, endings, death, darkness, quietness, and the sky' (Darvill 1997, 189).

Other evidence can be usefully considered. A recent study by Josh Pollard and Clive Ruggles (2001) looked at the range of materials intentionally placed within the early ditch of Stonehenge and its Aubrey Holes. Deposits of worked flint, antler, animal bone and carved chalk, along with perhaps one human cremation, were placed on either side of both main entrances and within a limited area of the south-east sector of the ditch. A similar pattern is seen in Phase 2, during which groups of articulated animal bone and pieces of disarticulated human bone were incorporated with increasing frequency. This phase is also characterised by a large number of cremated human bone deposits, some placed in small pits cut into the tops of the Aubrey Holes and accompanied by a restricted range of specialised artefacts. The distinctive spatial distribution of the material, about which more will be said in the following chapter, was taken by the authors as indicating a concern during the monument's earliest phase with a quadripartite division based on the position of the sun during the midsummer and midwinter solstices, echoing Darvill's suggestions for the

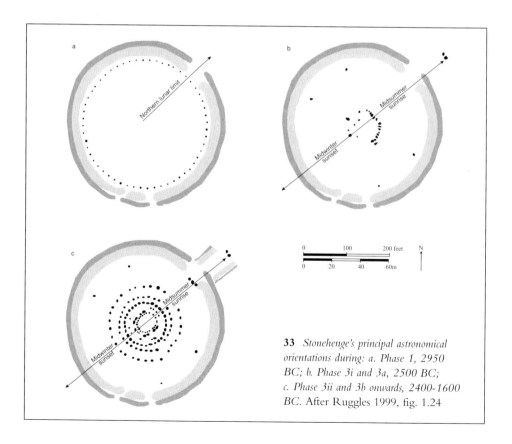

33 *Stonehenge's principal astronomical orientations during: a. Phase 1, 2950 BC; b. Phase 3i and 3a, 2500 BC; c. Phase 3ii and 3b onwards, 2400-1600 BC. After Ruggles 1999, fig. 1.24*

34 *Looking north-eastwards from the inside of Stonehenge and towards the Heel Stone.* Copyright courtesy of Bob Johnston

wider landscape. This contradicts the widely held view that it was only with the site's later rebuilding that solar symbolism became important, the earliest enclosure connected instead with the moon. But Pollard and Ruggles do not completely disregard the importance of lunar symbolism, noting that the clustering of the Phase 2 human cremations and other remains to the south-east of the monument corresponds to the direction of moonrise close to its southern extent, suggesting 'that solar- and lunar-derived cosmological schemes were not mutually exclusive' (Pollard & Ruggles 2001, 87).

There is, then, a strong possibility that celestial phenomena played some part in the religious beliefs and practices of at least one region during the later Neolithic. The available evidence can be best classified as indicating low-precision astronomical alignments and we should certainly not imagine anything akin to today's sophisticated science, with its imperative for producing a highly accurate body of astronomical knowledge. These imprecise, yet dramatic, alignments can be best understood if we consider that Neolithic peoples – just like many, if not virtually all, non-Western societies – saw celestial phenomena from a symbolic or religious point of view, the sky being invested with supernatural power and holiness, a place where spirits and maybe even gods dwelt. Given this, it is very easy to imagine how alignments towards heavenly bodies, such as the

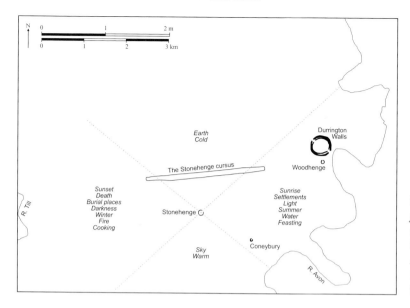

35 *The sacred geography of the Stonehenge landscape.* After Darvill 1997, fig. 7, table 3

sun and moon as they move regularly above and below the horizon, could quite easily be taken, during propitious occasions, as expressions of continuity or renewal. A correspondence between these events and the alignment of a monument would have created quite an impact during the ceremonies under-taken within the site. They would have added to the spectacle and emphasised to the onlookers that their world, just like that of the spirits in the sky, went round and round. At the heart of later Neolithic religion, as with so many others, may have therefore been the theme of regeneration.

The renewal of the world

The importance of regeneration has been highlighted by what many professionals describe, somewhat laconically, as the 'fringe' of archaeology – writers such as Michael Dames (1977) and Terrence Meaden (1999). What these two have in common is a belief that henge monuments were intrinsically linked to the worship of a Mother Goddess. A focus for their work has been the famous monument of Avebury, in Wiltshire, whose massive ditch and bank surrounded an outer circle of ninety-eight standing stones and two smaller inner circles (**5** & **colour plate 2**). Both see the layout of the monument as revealing its role as a high temple to a Mother Goddess, complete with genital shrines or wombs within which a cosmic marriage took place with a Sky Father. As Dames describes, the monument was 'built to provide a communal May festival wedding ring, shaped as a living image of the goddess as Bride, pictured in union with her male consort . . . . The temple was designed to reveal the shape of the Great Goddess, on a scale big enough to be occupied or "known" by large worshipping congregations' (1977, 123). To him, the site is a physical representation of this very god and connected to the outside world by the West Kennet and Beckhampton Avenues (**36** & **colour plate 5**), or what he regards as serpents, an animal frequently connected around the world with human fertility. Dames therefore considers that 'the entire structure was originally conceived as alive, an organism drawing its life from the vital spirit of the landscape' (1977, 124-5).

Both authors make the most of the oft-repeated statement that Avebury's standing stones possess sexual characteristics and may thus be linked with fertility. The taller and thinner megaliths, sometimes with more or less parallel sides and standing erect, are seen as resembling phalluses, and consequently gendered as male, whilst the shorter, squatter stones are their female counterparts (**37**). Along the West Kennet Avenue, which runs from Avebury's south entrance for nearly 1½ miles (2.3km), these 'male' and 'female' stones are even sometimes paired off against one another. Terrence Meaden (1999) has gone further, arguing that many of their natural outlines show human heads, usually in profile, and always with an eye. In most cases these are left-sided, which is, according to the writer, universally associated with femininity – they are therefore seen as depicting women's heads, and he notes, with great interest, the western British folk tradition of megaliths being maidens transformed into stone. The link with femininity and the Mother Goddess is also regarded as irrefutable because the lozenge-shaped and angular 'female' stones at Avebury are all based upon the triangular shape, or what is considered as a universal symbol of the vulva and pubic zone. Indeed, one particular stone within the southern inner circle, its surface covered in natural grooves and wrinkles, is

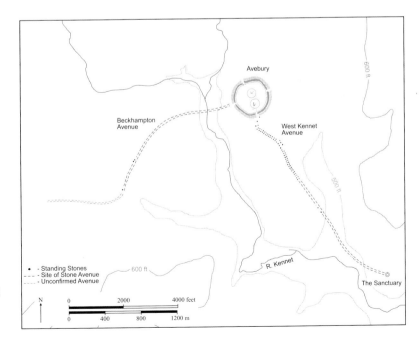

36 *The location of Avebury and its two stone avenues*

37 *Example of a large 'female' stone at Avebury, Wiltshire*

apparently a dead ringer for female genitalia, especially significant since the only tall thin stone at Avebury (described by Stukeley as 'the Obelisk' in the eighteenth century, but since destroyed) once stood nearby, this 21ft (6.4m) long pillar casting a phallic shadow across the vulva-marked stone with the rising sun on May Day (Meaden 1999, chapter 3). Similarly, the Cove, a distinctive rectangular setting of three stones (of which only two now survive) within the northern inner circle (**colour plate 7**), faces the midsummer sunrise so that the sun's rays would have penetrated its opening (Meaden 1999, chapter 8).

The interplay between stone, sunlight and shadow is regarded as a symbolic representation of the Sky God and Earth Goddess marrying and mating at the beginning of time (a theme to which I shall shortly return), the monument's builders and users thereby 'reassuring themselves of the future success and prosperity of their hopefully fertile but uncertain world' (Meaden 1999, 24). These 'would have been joyous events in the lives of the worshippers. The festival may have lasted a couple of days or more, to give enough time for a grand celebration and to allow for the arrival of a sunrise of clear sky' (Meaden 1999, 75). Dames (1977, 152-4) sees the massive Obelisk at Avebury as the ultimate phallic image, indeed as the ancient precursor to the maypole, which interestingly enough, was erected next to the original position of this standing stone during the nineteenth century. Expanding colourfully on his idea that the site was a communal May festival wedding ring, he speculates that 'Since marriages are made to be consummated, we can assume that love-making took place somewhere within the Avebury enclosure, and where better than under the shadow of the Obelisk?' (Dames 1977, 154). A concern with fertility, marriage and consummation has also been applied to Stonehenge, where the long phallic-like shadow of the Heel Stone penetrates the inner sarsen stones, or the Earth Mother's genital shrine or womb, on the midsummer Solstice dawn (Meaden 1997): and a highly stylised carving on one of its uprights – consisting of a rectangular or squarish outline with a protuberance at the centre of its top side – has been interpreted as a goddess image on account of parallels with others in Brittany (Castleden 1993, 210-5).

One does not have to accept the detail of these arguments – and both writers are too uncritical in their use of the evidence – to concede they are surely right to emphasise the importance of fertility, or indeed, that Neolithic peoples believed life itself was dependent on supernatural forces. This would account for the construction of enclosures whose very shape personified the notion of circularity and renewal, particularly if the symbolism was connected to the sun and moon, as is perhaps illustrated by the astronomical orientation of Stonehenge, Coneybury and Woodhenge. These celestial phenomena would not be understood as they are rationalised today, as parts of the physical universe whose cycles through the sky could be reliably tracked by science. Instead, they were mysterious entities whose regular appearance, disappearance and reappearance was anything but taken for granted, hinging rather on people's success in following the beliefs and strictures of their own religion. The sun and moon being understood as the very phenomena on which life depended certainly explains why henges represented the outer world in microcosm. By so directly linking their landscape with these heavenly bodies, the builders were appreciating that the fecundity of the former was directly dependent on the latter. The acts of ritual undertaken within the enclosures were therefore an attempt to ensure that the landscape in which they lived was fertile – a place on which they could rely for sustenance for as long as they undertook the appropriate acts of homage.

If henge banks did indeed symbolise the physical rim of the known world, as suggested by Colin Richards, then these sites may celebrate the horizon's fusing together of sky and earth. This makes sense when we consider that fecundity is seen by many societies as dependent on a Sky Father and Earth Mother. To the pre-Hellenic Greeks, Mother Earth was broad-breasted Gaia, who gave birth to Ouranos, or the starry heaven, which in turn became her mate and whose semen populated the earth with gods and monsters until his youngest son, Kronus, cut off his genital organ and threw it into the seas. His place was taken by Zeus, whose name suggests he was an essentially celestial phenomenon, and who governed the storms, the rains and the winds, or the very sources of fertility. Amongst the Maori of New Zealand, the Earth Mother was known as Papa, and in the beginning she closely embraced her partner, Rangi the Sky, until her children cut the cords binding heaven and earth, pushed them apart, and created some breathing room on the planet's bosom. Very similar mythologies were also common throughout the Americas, as with the Indians of southern California, who believed there was Turkmit, the He Sky, and Tomaiyowit, the Earth Mother pregnant with all the world's First Peoples. If examples such as these provide analogies for the later Neolithic, then henge monuments could have served as gateways between this world and the transcendental qualities, power and changelessness of the sky. In short, they were the places where heaven communicated with the earth and where the world was renewed by celestial beings.

That fertility and reproduction was a concern during the Neolithic is hinted at by a small number of enigmatic chalk objects found at both causewayed enclosures and henge monuments from the southern English chalklands. There are often realistically carved chalk phalli, such as the rather immodest example from Maumbury Rings, in Dorset, measuring nearly some 9 inches (22cm) in length, and chalk and stone balls, interpreted by some as accompanying testicles (**38**). There are also chalk 'cups', too small to have served as drinking vessels or lamps, but quite plausibly seen as the female counterparts of the male organ. These objects are actually quite rare, with only Stonehenge I and Mount Pleasant producing more than a couple of examples, and their complete absence from Durrington Walls suggest they were not a universal feature of all chalkland henge monuments. Nevertheless, they could have served as symbols of fertility or rebirth, and it is possible that in the non-chalk areas of the British Isles similar objects were made out of less durable materials like wood. A surviving later Neolithic example is the remarkable hermaphroditic ashwood figure, the so-called 'god-dolly', discovered with a waterlogged wooden trackway in the

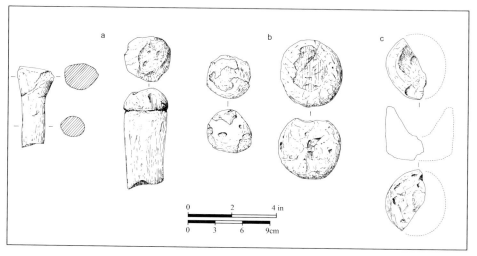

38 *Carved chalk phalli (a), balls (b) and cup (c) from Mount Pleasant, Dorset.* After Wainwright 1979, figs 75 & 77

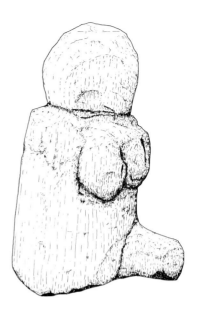

39 *The 'god-dolly' from the Somerset Levels.* After
Coles & Coles 1986, VII

Somerset fens. This hand-sized figure possesses both breasts and an extended
penis (**39**). It could even be argued that antler, found far more commonly on
both fourth and third millennium monuments and interpreted as digging
implements, could have sexual connotations, and were symbols of strength and
virility, their annual growth and shedding symbolising the cycle of regeneration.
The antlered stag skull placed near a chalk phallus in one of the shafts at
Maumbury Rings is particularly illuminating (Bradley 1976, 20), as are the relatively large number of antler found in the ditches flanking the northern
entrance of Stonehenge I, a location which has also produced four carved chalk
balls (Montague 1995a, fig. 218; Serjeantson & Gardiner 1995, fig. 229).

The fact that these objects are found at earlier monuments suggest that a
concern with fertility and reproduction was in fact not new. But recent
evidence does point towards the intriguing possibility that such beliefs may have
been brought sharply into focus on the eve of the third millennium. An ice-
core taken from Greenland shows a peak of sulphuric acid with a radiocarbon
date of 3150 ± 90 BC (3600-2900 BC). This is taken to indicate a volcanic
eruption, perhaps in Iceland, and the resulting dust-veils are seen as responsible
for a contraction in the width of the annual growth rings of English and Irish
oaks at 3195 BC (Baillie 1995, chapter 5; Baillie & Brown 2002, 501-4). The
more general impact on the British Isles can only be guessed at, but it seems
highly unlikely that there was no disruption, particularly when we consider
historically documented eruptions. It is even plausible that the effects were
disastrous. Early Chinese texts record how the Shang Dynasty's appearance
around 1600 BC was preceded by a catastrophic event, interpreted as a volcanic
eruption, whereby 'the earth emitted yellow fog . . . the sun was dimmed . . .

three suns appeared . . . frosts in July . . . the five cereals withered . . . thereby famine occurred' (Pang *et al.* 1989 quoted in Baillie 1995, 80). The end of the Shang, at around 1100 BC, may have coincided with a similar event: 'For 10 days it rained ashes, the rain was gray . . . it snowed in July . . . frosts killed the five cereals'. An eruption in Iceland in 1783 produced violent thunderstorms, flooding and clouds of ash and sulphurous gases in Britain. The sun was scarcely visible, trees shed leaves and crops were ruined. What followed was panic and fear, the first documented ghost stories and gothic novels. As Burl says, 'If these were the effects that the eruption had upon ordinary people only two centuries ago . . . how much more frightful must have been the reactions of prehistoric groups, incapable of understanding the calamity, existing in a fragilely capricious spirit-world, knowing only that their once-assured means of communicating with that world had failed' (2000, 30).

While it is no more than speculation, it is tempting to link the volcanic eruption with the religious 'revolution' described in chapter 1. Such a disaster would have provided an additional 'kick' to an already teetering system of ancestor cults. Rapidly changing climate, devastated crops and famine were a clear sign that the old ways had failed. What followed may have been the appearance of new beliefs and practices – or attempts to quite literally renew the world – and these could have been associated with the earliest 'formative' henges. As the effects of the volcanic eruption naturally subsided, the new cults were seen as answering people's prayers, as succeeding where traditional religion had failed. Their success may have even given rise to a belief in powerful supernatural beings who had interceded on the people's behalf, offering them spiritual deliverance. The henge phenomenon therefore took hold as more and more communities converted to the new religion. As already argued, their very design emphasised a concern with the renewal or the repro-duction of the world, their circular shape drawing on the cyclical movement of celestial phenomena, and similarly being without a beginning and without an end. The symbolism and experience of these monuments created a sense of stability and changelessness: for to enter these sacred arenas was to become at one with the timeless forces that controlled the cycle of birth, death and rebirth. And the potency of the association provided the monuments with long-term continuity in their design. They were to endure for over 500 years.

A concern with fertility, reproduction and renewal may account for another distinctive characteristic of the monuments. Henges are generally located in low-lying positions, on the floor of natural bowls or valleys, and many are sited in close proximity to water. The Stones of Stenness and the Ring of Brodgar are, as already mentioned, surrounded by open water, and one side of the Marden 'henge enclosure', in Wiltshire, is formed by the River Avon. There are also instances where henge ditches may have contained water for long periods of the year. Possibilities would include the two Orcadian henges, their ditch fills found to be in a waterlogged state; Milfield North and Milfield South in Northumberland, whose ditch fills contained the sorts of fine sediments that could have resulted from the inwash of rainwater; Bull Ring in the Peak District, where a thin layer of clay at the bottom of its ditch may have been deposited by water action; and Cairnpapple Hill in Lothian, where the glacial clay removed from the rest of the site but not from its ditch would have led to rainwater becoming trapped (Richards 1996). It has even been claimed that the massive flat-bottomed ditch at Avebury turned into a moat during the rainy season, although the excavation results do in fact contradict this interpretation (Gray 1934, 132-4). Furthermore, ground water occurred at a depth of nearly 10ft (3m) within the similarly large ditch at Marden, but the site's excavator suggested that the level of the water table must have been lower during the later Neolithic 'or else the digging of the ditch would have presented considerable difficulties' (Wainwright 1989, 65).

It is of course possible that such a close association with water was purely coincidental, and consequently meaningless – although the fact that a number of henge-related enclosures in Ireland encircle ponds and springs, whilst others were located near to deliberately created or natural ponds, suggests a far more purposeful link on at least one side of the Irish Sea (Condit & Simpson 1998, 59-61). But even if the association was accidental its symbolism may have been no less potent. Water represents a fundamental element in many non-Western religions. It guarantees the fecundity of people, animals and plants, and as noted, rain is often regarded as the seed of a Sky Father. There is nothing more

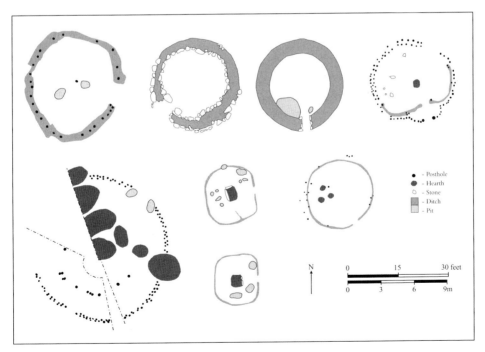

40 *A selection of later Neolithic houses.* After Darvill 1996, fig. 6.10

essential to living than water, yet its unpredictability and unbridled power can be a harbinger of suffering and even death. The flow of water is also a potent metaphor for movement or journeys, and it is commonly linked with social notions of purity and pollution. It is therefore more than possible that later Neolithic religion associated areas of water, such as rivers, springs and bogs with supernatural spirits, or even with a god-like being. Such a concern may be illustrated by other aspects of the later Neolithic evidence, notably the deposition, or sacrifice, of 'special' items like polished stone axes, and even human bone, into or near water, a practice which began during the fourth millennium and which was to continue for many millennia afterwards, including during the Christian Middle Ages.

Conclusion

Chapter 1 proposed that the widespread adoption of 'classic' henges, and all they represent, was a profound break with the past. Integral to the religious ideas that swept across parts of the British Isles was an emphasis upon what one archaeologist has recently described as 'the circular world' (Bradley 1998, chapter 7). This shared perception, or way of understanding the world, is best illustrated by the shape of these monuments, and their symbolism may have drawn inspiration from, and been directly linked to, the concepts of renewal, reproduction and rebirth. The circle was not therefore just a feature of design but a representation of sacredness itself. Not surprisingly, it permeated other aspects of third millennium life. There is now good evidence from at least some parts of the British Isles for a transformation in house shape. In England and Wales most early Neolithic structures are of rectilinear or squarish outline whilst the majority of later Neolithic structures are circular (**40**). There is a general absence of truly circular houses in Scotland, but a relatively large number of oval structures, largely from Shetland and Orkney, which date to the latter half of the fourth millennium and the third millennium. The evidence from Ireland is similarly complex, if more numerous, yet it is again possible to see the later adoption of circular house plans, as from around 3500 BC.

Nor is this 'circular world' illustrated merely by built sites. Its possible importance is also highlighted by later Neolithic art. Scattered across the hills and fells of the Peak District, northern England and Scotland are outcrops of natural rock whose surfaces had been carved and pecked by a series of largely curvilinear motifs, of which the cup mark and cup-and-ring are the most common (**41**). There are problems with dating this open air rock art, but some of the British and Irish passage graves are similarly decorated (**42**) – they are also embellished by an array of geometric motifs – and these belong to either the very late fourth millennium or very early third millennium. The rock art is consequently regarded as mainly a later Neolithic phenomenon, suggesting

41 *Cup-and-ring marks*

42 *Circular Irish passage grave art.* Copyright courtesy of Bob Johnston

43 *Spirals on Morwick Mill, Northumberland*

44 *Spirals on Long Meg, Cumbria.* Copyright courtesy of Nick Best

that the beliefs and practices which spread at the start of the third millennium also gave rise to a common style of art, and it is perhaps more than coincidence that it occurs in areas where henges are largely absent. The most distinctive link between the open air rock art and the passage graves is provided by the spiral, an obviously curvilinear motif which occurs, albeit very rarely, with the tombs and on specially selected stone, such as on the vertical river cliffs at Morwick Mill in Northumberland (**43**), or on the tall orthostat of Long Meg (**44**), located just outside a stone circle in Cumbria. The motif can also be found on Grooved Ware pottery and other later Neolithic objects like the carved stone balls of Aberdeenshire and other parts of Scotland. All this evidence, when considered alongside the appearance of henges and the changes in house design, suggest that seeing 'in the round' had indeed become a dominant theme of the later Neolithic 'world view'.

3

EXPERIENCING HENGE MONUMENTS

We wish to confront real people in real worlds, the inhabitants of what I call Hengeworld. I chose this term to avoid explicit reference to date, people, place, pottery styles or anything else with which archaeologists might choose to partition the past. It refers to that time and place when people were digging out the ditches and banks, cutting the trees for the massive circular timber circles and, on occasion, dragging huge stones into place.

Pitts (2000, 29)

. . . nearly all the different 'types' of monument found in the Late Neolithic and Early Bronze Age can be understood as interpretations of a circular archetype which reflects a more general perception of the world . . . such a development marks a significant threshold in the use of monumental architecture. It involves a change from the essentially private space of the tomb, to the creation of open arenas as a theatre for more public events.

Bradley (1998, 101)

Understanding space

The previous two chapters have explored the relationship between henge monuments and the development of a new world order or set of religious beliefs and practices. They emphasise the chronology and symbolism of these sites, and by doing so, give prominence to long-term generalities or historical processes. This is an approach which reflects the imperfections of the archaeological record and an understandable tendency on the part of prehistorians to view the past in centuries, rather than days and months, and as populated by societies, instead of individuals and small groups. Yet this viewpoint is unique to the archaeologist and fails to reflect the reality of those who built and used these monuments, for as the opening quotation implies, they understood their world through the immediacy, intimacy and physicality of human experience, which includes the bodily senses of sight, sound, touch and smell. Hence, it is necessary to complement the generalities of the previous chapters with an approach which grasps the day-to-day realities through which later Neolithic beliefs and customs would have been practised.

Henge architecture allows us to glimpse the reality of contemporary human experience. As is argued in the second quotation, their design involved a radical change in how religious or ceremonial space was experienced. A greater emphasis was now placed on creating an open arena for dedicated acts of public worship – as opposed to the cramped gloomy chambers of early Neolithic tombs – and given the size of many henge monuments it is likely that some saw large-scale participation and impressive audiences. A number of writers have even suggested that the bigger henge banks could have acted in much the same way as football terraces – as viewing platforms for spectators. Gray (1934, 161), when excavating Avebury, noted that 'Presumably the vallum served as elevated ground from which spectators could watch ceremonies in progress within the circle, without being allowed to go closer'. Such a use would have been made more effective by their circular, or near circular, design, a shape which maximised the visibility of any ritual by possessing a central point which all could see. It also goes some way towards explaining why ditches were dug inside the banks, for these could have then acted as a barrier between the viewing audience and those participating in the ceremonies, creating a distinction between the privileged 'insiders' and excluded 'outsiders'. In truth, their possible use as grandstands is only really applicable to the minority of sites with large banks, yet it is undeniably the case that all henge earthworks, like their inner timber settings or standing stones, would have ordered movement, encounter and interaction. In other words, the architecture of henge monuments impacted on the bodily experience of all involved in the spectacle of public worship irrespective of their vantage point.

I have already argued that the encircling earthworks of henge monuments create a place which is different or separate from the excluded landscape, quite literally lifting religious beliefs and practices out of everyday existence. For those moving towards, and into, these sacred arenas, the surrounding banks would signal a required change in their actions and movements, in the same way that passing through the walls of a church remind visitors to adopt a respectful manner, by speaking quietly and moving more slowly. This transformation in behaviour may have even occurred before the earthworks were reached. It is noticeable, for example, that both the massive 'henge enclosure' of Durrington Walls, and the much smaller site of Woodhenge (**45**), were situated in an area of landscape largely devoid of contemporary occupation. Fieldwalking has identified only low densities of surface lithics from their immediate vicinity, and this, when compared to far higher quantities less than

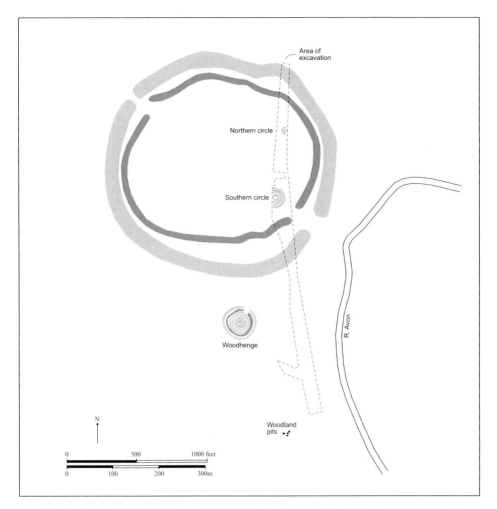

45 *Durrington Walls, Woodhenge and the Woodlands pit group.* After Wainwright 1971, fig. 2

a mile away, suggests how behaviour may have differed within sight of the monuments (Richards 1990, 269, fig. 158). This general absence of settlement is complemented by the Woodlands pit group, located immediately to the south of the two henges. They contained a range of 'special' items like unused axes and arrowheads, bone pins, and marine shells, reiterating the impression that people conducted themselves differently in the vicinity of Durrington Walls and Woodhenge. Ritual or ceremonial practice may have occurred just outside the two monuments.

Similar observations can be made around the three impressive and closely-spaced henges at Thornborough (Harding, J. 2000), located immediately to the east of the central Pennines in North Yorkshire. The majority of later Neolithic ploughsoil lithics from across the local landscape were a third of a mile or more away from the gravel plateau across which the monuments are sited (**46**), in areas where the topography breaks to form slight knolls, ridges and depressions. It is as if the plateau was kept clear of everyday occupation or other mundane activities as people undertook the celebrations and commemorations associated with the henges. The largest of the lithic concentrations was on the slopes of a low knoll known locally as Chapel Hill, half a mile to the east of the central henge. Interestingly, the rising relief of this low ridge blocks any view that people may have had of the plateau and its three remarkable henges, reiterating the distinctions being drawn across the wider landscape. People approaching the monuments would have had to pass from their areas of everyday occupation to the 'excluded space' of the flat gravel plateau, and this sense of crossing a threshold would be embedded in the changing topography and crystallised by the views of the henges which met the participants. The experience of the Thornborough landscape was therefore a journey from the normal parameters of life to a different and other world. It was the monuments which gave meaning to this journey. They were emotionally charged and visually impressive symbols, and the presence of the surrounding 'excluded space' suggests that their influence extended outwards, like a weakening gravitational field, across the landscape.

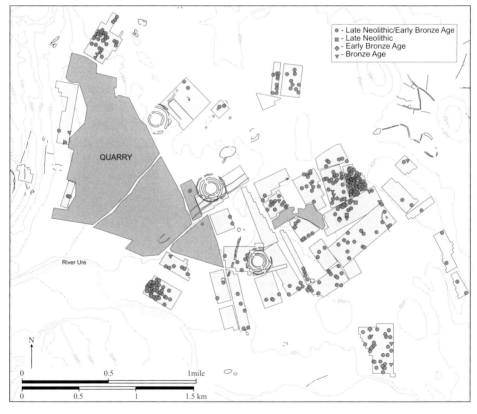

46 *Distribution of later Neolithic surface lithics at Thornborough*

The journey could be even more formally prescribed or orchestrated. The giant 'henge enclosure' of Avebury was connected to its surrounding landscape by the West Kennet and Beckhampton Avenues (**36**), the former consisting of two roughly parallel rows of stones about 50ft (15m) apart. These are truly impressive constructions, both being over 1½ miles in length, and while the Beckhampton Avenue is largely destroyed, the West Kennet Avenue most likely consisted of no fewer than a hundred pairs of stones (**colour plate 5**). They mark a formal route to the southern and western henge entrances, and the presence of worn chalk discovered during excavations at the West Kennet Avenue suggests that people moved along the lines of the stones or just outside the rows. They are therefore seen as processional routeways which structured the approach to Avebury, their impact on human experience most vividly demonstrated by the fact that the henge is hidden from view along most of the length of the West Kennet Avenue. It is only at a point some 330ft (100m) from its southern entrance, as the avenue reaches the top of a low ridge over-looking the natural basin in which the site is located, that the henge fully reveals itself. The sense of surprise and wonderment by those following the stone rows must have been palpable, and at such a moment these people may have changed their way of behaving. It is no more than speculation, but perhaps they, just like the modern visitor to a Christian church, lowered their voices, and began to move slowly and quietly. Alternatively, they perhaps became frenzied, proceeding quickly and rhythmically to the beat of a drum. Either way, the avenue was the perfect 'mood setter'. Its physicality not only controlled movement, encounter and interaction, but played an important role in changing people's emotional outlook.

Boundaries and thresholds

Movement through these surrounding landscapes assured that people arrived at the monuments in an appropriate frame of mind. Their senses were now sharply focused on the communal rites of thanksgiving and supplication soon to commence. They may have been excited, or even apprehensive, about what lay ahead, and the sheer monumentality of some henge banks – which were often larger on either side of the causeway – would have heightened their emotions as they approached and crossed into the sites. It was as much as a 100ft wide and some 10ft high at the massive 'henge enclosure' of Durrington Walls, and a possible revetment of large timbers may have given parts of its circuit a vertical outer face (Wainwright & Longworth 1971, 13-8, 196). The bank at Avebury, shown in **colour plate 2**, was of similar width, and remark-ably, still survives to a height of 14-18ft (4.2-5.4m). There is evidence that its inner extent was in places contained by a walling of chalk blocks, while a revetment of wooden uprights flanked the causeways (Smith 1965, 194-5).

The surfaces of its narrow entrances had even been reduced by scraping the top of the natural chalk, so that the banks at either side appeared higher and more impressive. Crossing one of these must have been an unforgettable experience, akin to moving between two steeply-sided cliff faces, and the banks, when first constructed, gleamed white from the chalk from which they were built. On a sunny day the effect could have quite literally dazzled those making the journey.

It was not just the giant 'henge enclosures' of the Wessex chalkland whose banks were fashioned for maximum impact. Mayburgh, located in the Cumbrian lowlands near to Penrith, has a huge bank of water-worn cobbles probably removed from shoals in the nearby River Eamont (Topping 1992, 249-53). It is still between 111-48ft (33.7-45.0m) wide and 12-24ft (3.8-7.3m) high, enclosing an area some 295ft (90m) across, and here, as with elsewhere, the bank was broader and higher on either side of the site's single causeway (**47**). To the east of the Pennines the grandeur of Mayburgh's construction is matched by the three massive henges located at Thornborough. These earthworks have been badly disturbed, but part of the central henge's bank survive to a width of nearly 60ft (18m) and a height of about 10ft (3m), rising to 14½ft (4.5m) on one side of its southern entrance (**48**). Visitors to Mayburgh and Thornborough would have been in no doubt as to the importance of what they were about to do as they moved towards and through their impressive earthworks. Both sites must have been awe-inspiring, as they are today, and their enclosing circuits originally possessed an unnatural brightness and intensity, achieved at Mayburgh by the colours of the river pebbles which made up its bank, and at Thornborough by its earthwork being possibly coated in white-coloured gypsum (Thomas 1955), a hydrated form of calcium sulphate which occurred locally.

47 *View of Mayburgh's entrance from outside the monument.* Copyright courtesy of Nick Best

1 *The most famous of monuments – Stonehenge, Wiltshire*

2 *The truly monumental 'henge enclosure' of Avebury, Wiltshire*

3 *The Stones of Stenness, Orkney.* Copyright courtesy of Richard Welsby

4 *The Ring of Brodgar, Orkney.* Copyright courtesy of Sue Scoones

5 *The West Kennet Avenue at Avebury, Wiltshire*

6 *The outer stone circle of Avebury, Wiltshire*

7 *The Cove at Avebury, Wiltshire*

8 *A virtual reality reconstruction of the view into Avebury from its southern entrance. The Obelisk can be seen towering above the other standing stones.* Copyright courtesy of Glyn Goodrick

9 *A virtual reality reconstruction of the view southwards from within Avebury's southern inner stone circle. The Obelisk and 'Z' feature dominate the setting.* Copyright courtesy of Glyn Goodrick

10 *A virtual reality reconstruction of the view southwards from outside Avebury's northern inner stone circle. The Cove dominates the setting.* Copyright courtesy of Glyn Goodrick

11 *Looking into the Milfield North henge reconstruction, Northumberland.* Copyright courtesy of Peter Forrester

12 *The lintelled outer stone circle at Stonehenge*

13 *A trilithon at Stonehenge*

14 *The enclosed area of Woodhenge, Wiltshire, with concrete markers where timber posts once stood*

15 *The Thornborough monument complex, North Yorkshire. The northern henge is covered by the copse of trees and alongside the southern henge is the excavation of a double pit alignment.* Copyright English Heritage

48 *The southern entrance of Thornborough's central henge from outside the monument*

Other features physically emphasised the act of crossing from the outside world into the enclosed space of the monuments. A number of excavated sites have produced evidence for structural features placed either within, or just outside, their entrances. A single standing stone was situated within the north-west causeway of Balfarg, Fife (Mercer 1981, 70-1); two allegedly flanked the northern entrance of King Arthur's Round Table (Topping 1992, 257), a site located near to Mayburgh; and a number are likely to have been placed across at least one of the two entrances to Arbor Low in the Peak District (Barnatt 1990, 31). Timber posts served the same purpose, as with the inferred pair of uprights within the ditch terminal of the eastern entrance at Devil's Quoits, Oxfordshire (Barclay *et al.* 1995, 21, fig. 14), or those erected in the causeway of the small henge at Gorsey Bigbury, Somerset (Harding & Lee 1987, 261-2). These simple features heightened the drama of crossing into the sites, something taken to the extreme at Stonehenge, where, around the middle of the first half of the third millennium BC, a complex arrangement of timbers was added to its north-eastern entrance (Cleal 1995b, 140-6). Their layout is open to interpretation, but is likely to have included eight rows of posts running roughly parallel to the side of the causeway, with a further four posts set in a line just outside the entrance (**49a**). They suggest the highly orchestrated control of movement into and out of the site, visitors having to pass through two narrow corridors barely 3ft wide and flanked by the uprights. These wooden settings were then replaced, between 2550-1600 BC, by three large standing stones just inside the entrance; a pair of stones, including the Heelstone, within a circular ditch outside of the enclosure; and the Avenue, comprising a pair of parallel banks, with quarry ditches on their outer sides, running in its entirety for over 1½ miles (Cleal 1995c, 268ff). They again illustrate the control of access through the site's north-eastern entrance (**49b**).

The experience of crossing into henge monuments was also enhanced by the inner ditch, which was occasionally separated from the bank by a wide berm (**28**), done deliberately perhaps to accentuate the journey from the outside to the inner sacred arena. Like the enclosing earthwork they could be impressive in size and more physically imposing around the entrances. At a number of excavated sites, the ditch is certainly wider and deeper on either side of the causeway: at the 'henge enclosure' of Marden, in Wiltshire, it expanded to 59ft (18m) wide and about 10ft (3m) deep instead of the more normal 52½ft (16m) and 6½ft (2m) respectively (Wainwright 1971, 185-7), whilst two of the three excavated terminals at the double-entrance site of Arbor Low were deeper than elsewhere around its circuit (Gray 1903). The ditches could also be more regularly dug-out around their entrances, suggesting, perhaps, that greater care was taken when building this part of the site. It could commonly possess squared-off, and sometimes steep-sided, terminal ends, thereby adding to the impression that people were moving across an abruptly bounded and significant threshold. The ditch at Mount Pleasant, for example, was ordinarily dug as a series on intersecting pits, but around two of its entrances it consisted of a more regular flat-bottomed trench between 23-48ft (7-14.5m) wide and as much as 10ft (3m) deep (Wainwright 1979, 35-47).

The significance of either entering or leaving a henge is demonstrated by the acts of deposition sometimes undertaken around this threshold. The ditches flanking the causeways were often the only part of the site where material

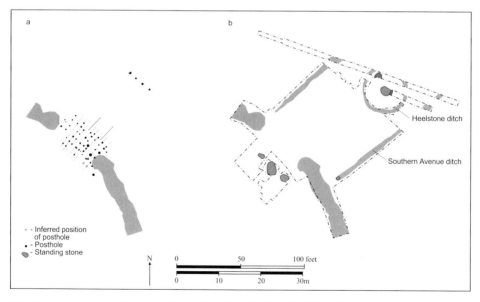

49 *Stonehenge's entrance features during a. Phase 2 and b. Phase 3.* After Cleal *et al.* 1995b, fig. 68; 1995c, fig. 156

culture or other remains were deliberately placed. There are few finds from the excavated ditch of Arbor Low, but its different terminal ends contained a small amount of worked flint – including six large jet black flakes placed deliberately on a ledge on the side of the ditch-butt – and a number of antler ties, an ox humerus and thirteen scattered ox teeth (Gray 1903, 468ff). Hearths and rede-posited spreads of ashy and burnt material were found in the terminals flanking both entrances at Devil's Quoits (Barclay *et al.* 1995, 14-20). There were fragments of burnt bone and dumped organic material in the excavated ditch ends at the two southernmost entrances of Milfield North, in Northumberland, perhaps the remains of cremation burials (Harding 1981, 108). Similarly, at Gorsey Bigbury a disturbed stone cist, with two individuals and a number of associated artefacts, was found in the bottom of the ditch just to the west of its single entrance, and at the other side of this gap a substantial deposit of what was interpreted as occupation material overlay the primary silting (Harding & Lee 1987, 261). Even more complex patterns are evident at the recently excavated Wyke Down, in Dorset, and it is the pits dug out on either side of the single entrance which have produced the majority of carved chalk objects, Grooved Ware pottery and human bone (Bradley *et al.* 1991, 96-101).

But it is again Stonehenge which provides some of the most elaborate evidence for acts of deposition in and around entrances. Material was frequently placed in the eastern half of both its ditch and the inner Aubrey Holes, but the ditch-ends were the favoured location for a wide range of remains deposited throughout the third millennium BC (Cleal *et al.* 1995; Pollard & Ruggles 2001). The worked flint, known to be concentrated around the entrances, was probably associated with the site's construction, but the distribution of other categories of material may have been more mean-ingful. The carved chalk objects likely to date to this period – of which roughly-shaped balls are the most common – were mainly from around the site's north-eastern and south-western entrances (**50a**), whilst the small number of bone or antler objects in the ditch, including finely worked pins, were also placed near entrances (**50b**). The pattern is partly repeated by the more numerous antler picks and rakes, a relatively large number being deposited to one side of the northern entrance and around the southern entrance (**50c**), and by animal bone, with partially complete skeletons, cattle skulls and mandibles in particular found near to the entrances. The majority of burnt human bone in the ditch – the remains of cremation burials – were associated with the terminals to one side of the north-eastern and southern entrances, while unburnt disarticulated bone, including skull fragments, were clustered around the northernmost of these causeways (**50d**). The evidence, when taken together, suggests carefully orchestrated depositional practices, particularly as people moved in and out of the main north-eastern entrance, and patches of burning were also noted on the ditch bottom to either side of this causeway, in one instance with a heap of scorched antler picks.

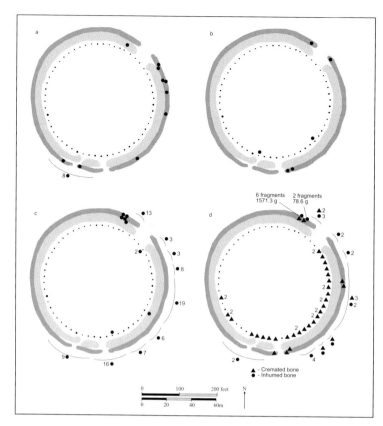

50 *The distribution of deposited material at Stonehenge: a. chalk objects, b. bone and antler objects, c. antler picks and rakes, and d. human bone.* After Montague 1995a, fig. 218; 1995b, fig. 225; Serjeantson & Gardiner 1995, fig. 229; McKinley 1995, fig. 250

If henge earthworks were indeed a symbolic barrier between the 'purity' of their inner arenas and the 'impurity' of the excluded landscape, then the placing of objects and other remains in terminal ditches may have been a poignant and dramatic act. One way of understanding these deposits is to see them as bids to deliberately link the realities of everyday existence with the powers and agencies of later Neolithic religion. They could each represent important aspects of people's lifeways: the dumps of burnt or ashy material the importance of fire to everyday living; the flint, which was either collected or quarried from the ground, the fecundity of the earth on which all depended; the antler and carved chalk 'cult' objects the role of fertility and mating to earthly success; the animal bone the food, pelts and hides which were essential to being alive; and human bone the ghostly ancestors who stalked human existence and granted or withheld goodness as they saw fit. All these deposits could have been attempts to bargain with the supernatural, offerings of thanks and appeasement, or responses to specific problems and crises such as death, illness or crop failure. By placing these material sacrifices in the ground, people may have believed they were assuring their own destiny – their health, fertility and wealth. This could even account for the great depth of many henge ditches, reflecting the wish to penetrate the sacred earth for the dedication of these gifts.

The inner world of henge monuments

Henge earthworks physically emphasised the interior of the sites. The arrangement of outer bank and inner ditch orientated the gaze of anyone crossing these perimeters inwards, focusing their attention upon the enclosed space. The sensation of moving into a defined spatial arena would have been exasperated by the large size of some henge banks (**51 & 52**), which, as noted earlier, either completely restricted the view of the outside world or limited it to the rising relief of the surrounding landscape. Such closure is evident from within Thornborough, where it is not thought to have been possible to see the ridge immediately to the east of the complex, despite it rising to a height of 443ft (135m), and the more distant Hambleton Hills, nearly 10 miles away but visible on a clear day, would also be blocked from view. Alternatively, the chalk ridges which surround the giant henge monument of Avebury would have been evident at various places from within its interior, but their profile continues the line of the bank where it is hidden from view, as though adopting the role of the earthwork (Watson 2001, 302). If the outside world was being banished from the awareness of those gathered inside Thornborough, then this merging together of bank and skyline had the same effect. The care of people was firmly fixed on what was about to be undertaken within both sites.

The layout of their interiors further animated people's attention. The enclosed space of many henges contain a series of built features which, whilst ranging greatly in their structural appearance, can be divided into two basic types: the pits, postholes, and more rarely, rectangular or circular stone structures found in the centre of henge interiors: and the timber, stone and pit circles built around the inner circumference of these sites and usually concentric with the inside edge of the enclosure ditch. The two sets of features are know to co-exist at many monuments, so they are in no way mutually exclusive, and both would have divided the naturally undifferentiated circular area of these sites into a series of spaces, creating more complex opportunities for distinguishing and classifying between people and activities. They would have certainly created contrasting patterns of movement, visibility and hearing for people within the monuments, especially if they encompassed either a large part or their entire inner area, effectively dividing the enclosed space into regions of disclosure and hiddenness. Those visiting Avebury through its southern entrance, for example, would have been denied a clear view of the centre by the two enormous megaliths placed just inside its ditch and the standing stones of its inner southern circle (**colour plate 8**). These objects would create 'the illusion of a solid wall or some kind of building' (Watson 2001, 302). By contrast, those standing at the site's centre would be able to view the entire interior of the henge as the ground gradually drops away towards its enclosing earthwork.

51 *View of Mayburgh's entrance from inside the monument.* Copyright courtesy of Nick Best

52 *The inside of Thornborough's central henge*

The central features of henge monuments range greatly in their complexity. At one end of the spectrum are those sites with a small number of either pits, timber posts or standing stones. Examples would include Milfield North and Milfield South in Northumberland, where large-sized pits were excavated in the interiors, at the former within a pit circle (**53**). The steep-sided and flat-bottomed pit off-centre of Milfield South was over 6ft (1.9m) deep, contained a rectangular stone setting and a substantial post, and was surrounded by a number of very small dug features (Harding 1981, 93-100). The three grave-sized pits at the centre of Milfield North were furnished with stone packing above two upright slabs, what was possibly a wooden frame or coffin, and a likely charred plank, while a further pit, towards the south-west, contained a stone-built but empty cist (Harding 1981, 101-15). Other forms of central features are evident at Devil's Quoits, where a group of small postholes were all that remained of what must have been a modest structure (Barclay *et al.* 1995, 42-3), and across the inner area of Coneybury Hill, a site near to Stonehenge, were pits – some of which originally contained timber uprights – and dense clusters of stake holes, neither forming a discernible pattern (Richards 1990, 130ff). These may have all been structurally straightforward or small-scale additions but they nonetheless acted as foci for people congregating within the monuments. That they played a key role in acts of commemoration and worship is borne out by their association with deliberately placed material, such as the worked flint, pottery, bone fragments and a cup-marked block of sandstone found in the pit fills at the two Milfield sites.

Elsewhere these central features resemble a stage or impressive backdrop for the rituals undertaken within the sites. Both inner stone circles at Avebury enclosed distinctive orthostatic arrangements (Smith 1965, 198-202). At the centre of the southern circle was the Obelisk, the tallest of the erected stones with a height of 21ft (6.4m), described by some as a giant phallic symbol. Immediately to one side was a 85ft (26m) long alignment of twelve smaller stones known as the 'Z' feature (**54 & colour plate 9**). Inside the northern circle, by contrast, was the Cove, its three large stones, some of the biggest used at Avebury and as much as 16ft (4.8m) wide and high, defining what is basically a roofless sentry box (**colour plate 10**), open to the north-east and allegedly facing the moon's most northerly rising. Both these central features were places set aside, and consequently made special, in which the participants of any ritual could congregate. Their orthostats not only emphasised the importance of the ceremonies with which they were associated, but provided a focal point for the audience gathered around the surrounding circle of stone. People may have looked on, in the same way that theatre-goers observe a stage, the Cove even perhaps being used as a place of secrecy and mystery to which the chief participants could withdraw at strategic moments. It has also been suggested that the two inner circles were particularly well suited for the reflection of sound (Watson 2001, 308). At the Obelisk these activities included the excavation of four pits within which fine dark brown soil had been deposited. If this giant pillar was indeed a phallic symbol, then could they symbolise the fertility that people so desired?

Comparable, if much smaller, structures have been recorded elsewhere and are similarly surrounded by a stone circle. Two examples suffice to make the point. At the centre of Arbor Low at least six stone orthostats formed a rectangular setting approximately 10ft (3-4m) from side to side, the two largest originally standing to a height of over 9ft (2.7m) and facing the henge entrances (Barnatt 1990, 34-8). Known also as 'the cove', it, like Avebury, was supposedly aligned towards the maximum position of the moon. Excavations in and around the central feature found an extended skeleton and the ulna of another, but there is no evidence that these were contemporary

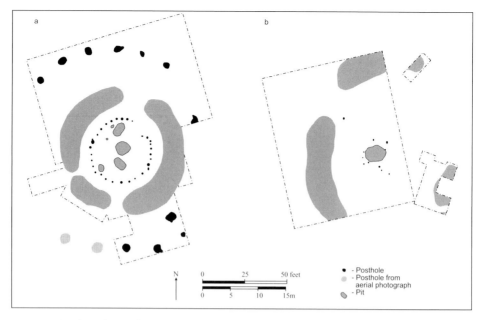

53 *Plans of a. Milfield North and b. Milfield South.* After Harding 1981, figs 5 & 12

with the earthwork or its stone settings. Similarly, at the Stones of Stenness three orthostats, of which only two are original, were located along the axis of the monument's centre and its single entrance (**55**). They were found with a range of other inner features, including a square setting of four large stone blocks placed into the ground at the site's centre and surrounding a timber upright; between this feature and the three orthostats was an area of stone paving, a pair of large stone holes and some form of four-post structure; and to the other side of the central feature a group of five pits (Ritchie 1975-6, 12ff). These form a linear foci, stretching from the henge entrance, for activity within the monument, although all or some of the features may post-date the construction of the henge and the excavator thought it unlikely they were contemporary.

Brief mention has already been made of the other type of enclosed features – the timber, stone and pit circles found around the circumference of these sites and usually concentric with the inner edge of the enclosure ditch. These varied greatly in their monumentality and at one end of the spectrum are a number of modestly sized circles. The ring of thirty pits within Milfield North (**53a**) was only 36ft (11m) in diameter and there is no evidence they ever contained uprights (Harding 1981, 108-9). Evidence for the erection of timbers was found, however, at Arminghall, Norfolk (Clark 1936), and North Mains, Perth and Kinross (Barclay 1983), both encircling an area about 82ft (25m) across (**23**). The eight posts at Arminghall were each up to 3ft (0.9m) in diameter and the twenty-four at North Mains between 1-2ft. Larger in size was the single ring of pits at Stonehenge, where the fifty-six Aubrey Holes, dug around the inside edge of the bank and encircling an area about 285ft (87m) across, held timbers on average about 3ft in diameter (Cleal 1995a, 95-107). It is impossible to prove the actual height of the timber uprights at each of these sites, but if we take the depth of the postholes, and apply a formulae whereby for every foot buried in the ground as much as three-and-a-half could be standing above the surface, then they could have been on average 10ft (3m) tall at Stonehenge, 15ft (4.5m) tall at North Mains, and staggeringly, as much as 26ft (8m) tall at Arminghall. Each of these circles must have been an extraordinary sight and if any of the timbers had been carved or painted – as with the totem poles of native Americans – they would have been even more striking (**colour plate 11**).

The smaller of the stone circles is similarly impressive. The interior of Arbor Low originally contained an oval of between forty-one and forty-three stones surrounding an area 121ft (37m) by 138ft (42m). The site is unique in that the orthostats are in a recumbent position, but it has been suggested that they were once upright (Barnatt 1990, 33-8). If so, they would have stood to about head height, although they may have been taller around the southern entrance where it is estimated that four stones were 8½-9½ft (2.6-2.9m) high. Equally splendid are the vertically set stones within the two Orcadian henges. The largest of these was the Ring of Brodgar (**colour plate 4**), originally consisting of between fifty-

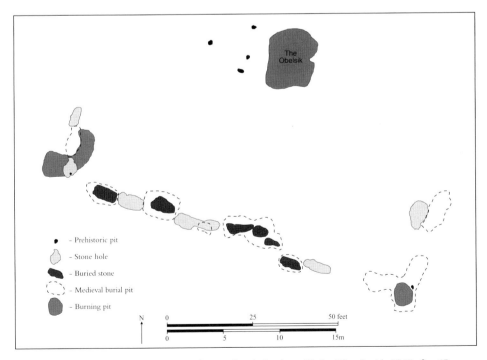

54 *The Obelisk and 'Z' feature within Avebury's Southern Circle.* After Smith 1965, fig. 65

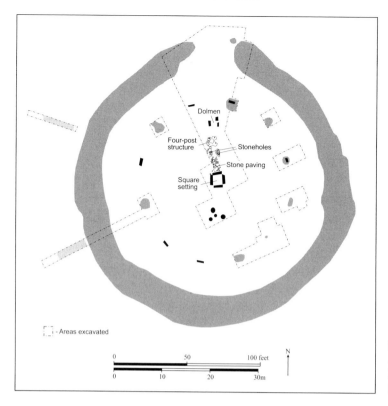

Dolmen

Four-post structure

Stoneholes

Stone paving

Square setting

☐ - Areas excavated

0   50   100 feet

0   10   20   30m

N

55 The *Stones of Stenness.* After Ritchie 1975-6, figs 2 & 5

nine to sixty-six stones forming a circle some 341ft (104m) in diameter (Barnatt 1989, table 7). The orthostats of this magnificent stone circle have a mean height of over 9ft (2.8m). The nearby Stones of Stenness (**colour plate 3**) was, by comparison, relatively small, with only as many as twelve uprights in a circle just some 98ft (30m) across (Ritchie 1975-6). However, its unshaped pillars of flagstone more than make up for this by reaching heights of over 17ft (5m or more), their phallic-like appearance – including bevelled tops, the result of the stone's natural fracture – making these powerful symbols of fertility and repro-duction. Then, finally, consider the stone circle within the Devil's Quoits (Barclay *et al.* 1995, 24-42), far to the south in the Thames Valley. This oval setting of twenty-nine stones enclosed an area with a maximum diameter of 259ft (79m).

Yet all these remarkable timber and stone circles are far from being the largest known. I have already commented on the impressive multi-circuit wooden structures built at the Wessex chalkland monuments of Woodhenge, Mount Pleasant and Durrington Walls during the latter half of the third millennium BC. These are very similar to one another, consisting of either five or six concentric circles of postholes enclosing areas between 125-144ft (38-44m) in size (**56, 57 & 58**). These features originally held uprights of oak as much as 3ft across, and because they generally got thicker and higher towards the site's centre have been interpreted by some as stanchions for a roofed building. Geoffrey Wainwright (1971, 206), for example, sees the Southern Circle at Durrington Walls – whose construction required an estimated 260 tons of timber – to have possessed a solid outer wall, an outward sloping roof and an open central court. However, in a recent review of these monuments, Alex Gibson (1998, chapter 6) suggests that the balance of evidence points towards their interpretation as freestanding or lintelled timber circles. It is impossible to determine their original appearance with any certainty, but whether they were roofed or not, they were places in which people could congregate, a focal point for activities like feasting and the deposition of a range of objects and food remains (see below): one has only to consider the visual impact of a large numbers of closely-set uprights, some reaching heights of nearly 20ft (6m), to grasp their appeal. The pivotal role of these timber structures certainly accounts for their siting within the 'henge enclosures': the entrance of the circle at Mount Pleasant, which was located on the highest ground and surrounded by its own henge, faced the northern causeway of the encircling bank and ditch, and the Southern Circle at Durrington Walls was located just inside one of the site's entrances (**5**).

That such architectural elaboration was matched in stone is again best illustrated by the excavated henges of the Wessex chalkland. The earlier monument at Stonehenge, including its timber circle, was repeatedly remodelled between 2550-1600 BC by the addition of a number of complex stone settings (Cleal 1995c, chapter 7). The sequence starts with the erection of bluestones, brought

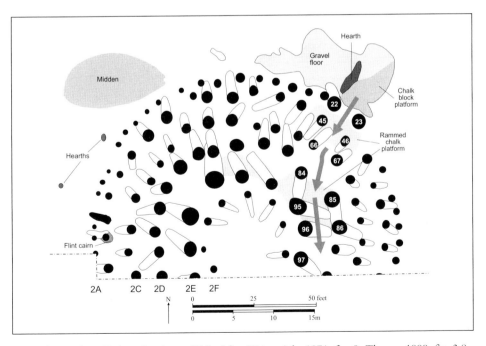

56 *The Southern Circle at Durrington Walls.* After Wainwright 1971, fig. 9; Thomas 1999, fig. 3.8

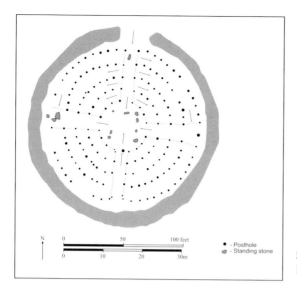

N

0   50   100 feet

0   10   20   30m

● - Posthole
◉ - Standing stone

57 *Site VI, Mount Pleasant.* After
Pollard 1992, fig. 8

all the way from south Wales, at the site's centre (**59a**), arranged into 'a semi-
circle, or even a three-sided, open rectangular form' (Cleal 1995c, 188).
Around 2400 BC, or the same time that the large multi-circuit timber structures began to be built elsewhere, they were dismantled and replaced by a circle
of thirty massive locally available sarsens, with connecting stone lintels along
their tops, and a similarly monumental inner setting of five trilithons, each with
two uprights and a horizontal lintel, formed into a horseshoe-shape (**59b**,
colour plates 12 & 13). Some time later a bluestone circle was erected
between the two sarsen settings, and an oval of bluestones added within the
trilithons (**59c**), its north-western arc subsequently removed to create a
horseshoe-shaped arrangement (**59d**). There is no doubting the monumentality of these successive phases of construction – the trilithons reaching heights
of over 22ft (7m) – and for anyone within the interior 'the overwhelming
impression gained is that the space is so enclosed, even in its ruined form, that
it feels like a building' (Cleal & Allen 1995a, 486). The awe and claustrophobia, still felt by visitors today, was surely a deliberate attempt to create a
place of secrecy and mystery, set aside from the outside world, within which
the appropriate rites could be 'safely' completed. The focal point may have
been the westernmost head of the inner horseshoe, astride the site's symmetry.
It faced the entrance, was framed by the largest of the trilithons, and was the
location of the so-called Altar Stone, a pillar of now partly buried Welsh
sandstone (**60a**). This part of the site can perhaps be best understood as a stage
for the chief participants in any acts of worship and supplication, the spectacle
made more dramatic if lit up by the early midsummer sun (**60b**).

No less awe inspiring are the stone circles constructed within Avebury. There
is uncertainty as to whether they were contemporary with, or later than, the
construction of its giant earthwork, but what is not in doubt is their sheer scale

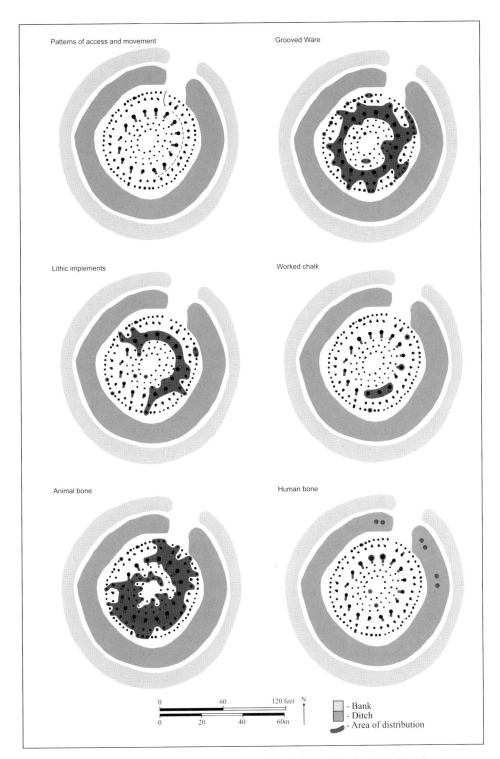

Patterns of access and movement

Grooved Ware

Lithic implements

Worked chalk

Animal bone

Human bone

0   60   120 feet   N

0   20   40   60m

☐ - Bank
☐ - Ditch
🌑 - Area of distribution

58 *Woodhenge and its deposited remains.* After Pollard 1995, figs 4-7, 9 & 12 and magnificence (**colour plate 6**). Some two hundred and forty-seven unshaped blocks of local sarsen, averaging about 15 tons in weight, were employed in the construction of its three circles. The outer circle of ninety-eight stones was over 1,000ft (329m) in diameter and the two almost perfectly round inner circles, probably consisting of twenty-seven and twenty-nine orthostats, were 320ft (97.5m) and 340ft (103.6m) across. Each of these represents a series of distinctive spaces through which people must pass if they are to witness or participate in the rituals undertaken around the Obelisk and the Cove. As a result, these focal points were buried 'deep' within the monument, becoming, as at Stonehenge, places of mystery and secrecy. This division of space may have also distinguished between activities and even people. Whilst there is no direct evidence, it is nonetheless tempting to associate different rites with each of the inner circles. If the Obelisk was indeed a phallic symbol, which cast its shadow across a vulva-marked stone on May Day (see chapter 2), then perhaps the southernmost of these circles was associated with fertility and regeneration. By contrast, some writers have linked the Cove with death and the ancestors on account of its similarities with the design of early Neolithic stone-built burial monuments. This, of course, is no more than speculation, but irrespective of their exact meanings the stone circles created a complex spatial liturgy.

The timber, stone and pit circles reiterate the circular design of henge monuments and the notions of wholeness and harmony with which they were associated. It is easy to imagine how those walking, or perhaps even dancing, their course would have been reminded of the repetitive and recurring qualities of their society, and its cosmos, as they went round and round. The importance of circular movement or procession has in fact been directly recognised at a number of the complex timber circles. The massive Southern Circle within Durrington Walls (Wainwright 1971, 23-38) had a wide entrance placed immediately opposite the surrounding enclosure's eastern causeway. It was flanked by the largest posts used in the structure and fronted by an irregular platform of chalk blocks and flint gravel (**56**). People passed over this threshold and, according to the distribution of laid chalk flooring, proceeded through the outer four circles, then turned left and moved around the inner two circles (Thomas 1999, 57-8). A similar pattern is evident at the comparable structure of Woodhenge, where, according to Josh Pollard (1995, 152), they may have moved straight through the two outer circles of posts and proceeded around the widest available gap, flanked on their inside by the largest timbers erected at the site (**58 & colour plate 14**). There could have been more complex access and movement at the combined henge and timber structure found within the large enclosure of Mount Pleasant, Dorset (Wainwright 1979, 22-8). A brief examination of its plan illustrates how the circles of posts were divided into equal quadrants by four corridors aligned on the cardinal points (**57**). However, the widest gap between its circuits is between the two outer rings, suggesting perhaps that people moved around the inside edge of the

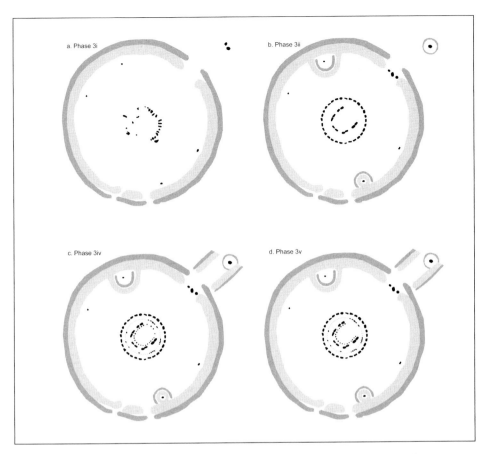

59 *The sequence of stone circle construction at Stonehenge.* After Cleal & Allen 1995a, figs 256-7

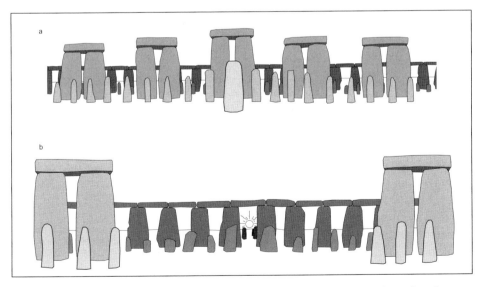

60 *Views from the inside of Stonehenge, reconstructed in true perspective from photographs: a. from the centre looking south-west, b. from the centre looking north-east.* After Castleden 1993, figs 89-90

timber structure and along the wide corridors which divide the site and lead to its central open area (Pollard 1992, 224-5).

These timber structures can therefore be likened to a circular maze which people navigated as part of the required ritual. Their movement was associated with the deposition of food remains and objects. I have already noted that henge entrances were often selected for specific act of deposition, but the same point can be made about other important thresholds or junctures in people's movement. The platform built at the entrance of Durrington Wall's Southern Circle was covered by the traces of extensive burning and a great quantity of Grooved Ware pottery, flints and animal bone. The excavator considered this to be 'a focal point outside the building proper where offerings were made and rituals performed prior to entering the structure itself' (Wainwright 1971, 216-7). Moreover, immediately to its north was a large oval hollow containing black ashy soil, huge quantities of pig bone, a great deal of Grooved Ware pottery, stone tools and some discarded bone pins (Wainwright 1971, 38-41). This was seen as the remains of a midden, or a place where rubbish from the activities associated with the Southern Circle's entrance was thrown. It highlights how the gathering of people outside the timber circle may have been an event of some magnitude, and the vast quantities of pig and cattle bone suggest large-scale feasting (Richards & Thomas 1984, 205-7). Acts of deposition were also undertaken as people moved through the structure. Deliberately broken pottery, flint, bone objects, and animal bone were all found in the tops of the massive postholes. These remains are also interpreted as offerings, either dropped or placed around the post bases while they were still standing. That they were the product of meaningful acts, and governed by a set of rules, is reiterated by the fact that there is a general fall-off in the density of material towards the centre of the site, and that the postholes containing the highest frequencies of flint flakes are those with relatively low quantities of Grooved Ware (Richards & Thomas 1984, figs 12.5 & 12.6).

Similar patterns of deposition are evident elsewhere. A recent study of Woodhenge by Josh Pollard (1995) records how the variety of material intentionally placed within the timber structure marked out its boundaries and thresholds. The distribution of Grooved Ware pottery, lithic implements, worked chalk and animal bone is densest in the postholes of the second and third circuits (58), between which people may have proceeded when the site was in use. Taken with the evidence from Durrington Walls, it suggests that codes governed where and how offerings could be made within timber circles. Far smaller quantities of remains were found within the inner henge of Mount Pleasant, but again they followed a distinct pattern (Wainwright 1979). The majority of the sixteen Grooved Ware sherds were either in the postholes of the two outer circuits, with most coming from its south-west quadrant, or from its central open space. These parts of the site must have been picked out for special treatment and it is noticeable that the more numerous pottery and flint concentrations found in the surrounding henge ditch were grouped in the north-west sector and opposite the timber structure's western corridor. Here, as at the other cited examples, there appears to have been a high degree of correspondence between people's potential routeways and the distribution of intentionally placed materials.

These acts of deliberate deposition may have been integral to the way people worshipped. A religious narrative or storyline was perhaps created by those journeying around the monuments, different parts of each site associated with specific meanings or connotations. By congregating in these areas, and sometimes completing acts of deposition, people were celebrating and reaffirming fundamental aspects of their beliefs. It is surely meaningful that the distribution of remains at Stonehenge and the nearby site of Woodhenge not only emphasised spatial thresholds but also what may have been key orientations. The lithics, pottery, human and animal remains, along with smaller assemblages of worked chalk and worked bone, are generally clustered on their eastern side, and whilst it can be objected that the western arc of Stonehenge's ditch is unexcavated, it is nevertheless the case that the Aubrey Holes in this half are more or less barren of deposits. This is perhaps unsurprising when we recall that all the nearby henges are located to the east of Stonehenge, and that, according to Darvill (1997, 189), the landscape's eastern quadrant was associated with 'sunrise, new beginnings, life, light, fertility, feasting, water, and the earth', the western quadrant, by contrast, linked to 'sunset, endings, death, darkness, quietness, and the sky'. By placing gifts, or offerings of thanks, on the eastern side of the monuments people may have been paying homage to the rising sun and acknowledging their debt to this life-giving power. This interpretation would also account for why, as discussed in the previous chapter, the distribution of intentionally placed material at Stonehenge is clustered around the midsummer and midwinter solstices, a pattern possibly repeated at Woodhenge, where every carved chalk object was found on an axis which 'related to a solar or lunar event' (Burl 1987, 126).

Conclusion

It is apparent that people's experiences of henges were structured or choreographed. Whether they entered these sites as large crowds, perhaps being led by their own religious leaders, or wandered in freely, with no one telling them what to do next or what to think, they behaved according to a set of preconditions. Learned ideas or concepts were the means by which these preconditions, or codes and beliefs, became the norm, but it was the physicality of the henge monuments, and their surrounding landscapes, which made these real, and consequently less forgettable. Analogies with modern day religions help us understand this process, despite the passage of thousands of years and beliefs completely alien to us today. If the overall layout of a Christian church, to take just one example, determines the routine of people, as they enter, move around, and position themselves, then the same is no less true of the later Neolithic monuments. If the former's altar provides a focus for the attending audience, then henges also had their own devices for focusing people's attention, whether they were pillars of stone or large posts. And if its cruciform-shape, stain glass windows and other ritual paraphernalia tell stories, then so does a henge's circular outline, its ditch and bank, their internal features, and the objects or residues found in and around these sites – stories about the world's inter-connectedness, about the relationship between people, their land and sky, and the elements upon which they depended.

To see henge architecture as presiding over a journey of spiritual renewal is to appreciate how people's experiences of these sites were inseparable from their moods and emotions. They could have come to the monuments at key moments in their lives, whether it was during a seasonal festival or on a holy day, during a wedding or coming of age ceremony, or at times of great social crisis. These occasions were times of emotion and drama, as they are today, feelings which would have been heightened by the henges themselves. By crossing the enclosing banks and ditches people left behind the realities and concerns of the everyday, finding themselves at a place where heaven and earth met, where they could speak to and bargain with the supernatural powers and agencies which ruled the cosmos. They may have assumed an altered state of consciousness during the journey and the religious symbols which festooned the insides of henges would have played with their feelings. These were made of well-known natural resources, yet their form and layout possessed an exotic-ness, stressing their special role in linking the earth with the sky. Orthostats that towered over their heads, pointing towards and impregnating the heavens, created a sense of wonderment, even dizziness, whilst more complex settings brought about confusion and claustrophobia, all adding to the impression of being in an 'other' world. But by moving around and making sense of these symbols people achieved a togetherness with their culture, grasping fully the fabulous, evocative and often dangerous possibilities which lay outside the henges – and with this knowledge came empowerment, intention and aspira-tion. In such a way they renewed the morality and spiritual well-being of themselves, their society, and the cosmos.

4

HENGE MONUMENTS, CEREMONY AND SOCIETY

. . . henges varied considerably in importance and represented a hierarchy of ceremonial construction.

Earle (1991, 91)

It is postulated that each level in the monument hierarchy may have functioned differently in the sense that they relate to varying levels of organisation within regional communities, ranging from monuments for local use by individual farming units, to regional centres which may have been gathering places for the majority of factions within a region.

Barnatt (1989, 166)

Understanding difference

So far I have discussed the henge monuments as if they were a unified phenomenon, a single class of site united by design, use and meaning. In fact, I have made a virtue of this, arguing that their circular or slightly ovoid layout, single or double entrances, and inner ditches and outer banks illustrate the widespread development of a standard architectural repertoire for ceremonial sites during the third millennium BC: and that the existence of shared features over such a large area could indicate 'that a similarity of intention was being expressed through this phenomenon' (Richards 1996, 331), thereby demonstrating an overarching set of religious beliefs and principles. Yet I now wish to change tack and confront an apparent contradiction in the evidence – for it is equally evident that henge monuments vary enormously in their size, the nature of their enclosing perimeters, and the presence or not of internal features. One has only to peruse the plans of individual monuments in previous chapters to gauge their many permutations, and published papers and books, including this one, talk of 'mini-henges', 'hengiforms' or 'henge enclosures', less than colourful terms by which to describe this variation.

How can we reconcile these all too apparent differences with their shared architectural repertoire and collective meaning? Of course, it could be argued that variation results solely from the chronological development of the sites, and chapter 2 demonstrated that the enclosing ditch of early monuments was often far more segmentary or interrupted when compared to later examples. Several authors have also suggested that entrance number could correlate with date, single-entrance sites often being earlier in the third millennium BC. However, this is difficult to prove given the small number of available radio-carbon determinations, and on present evidence it seems that single- or double-entrance sites co-existed during the later Neolithic. Therefore, when taken together, there is insufficient evidence that chronological change can in itself account for the variation that exists amongst henge monuments. There is certainly no indication that monuments got either smaller or larger as time passed, yet overall diameter is perhaps the most telling indicator of variation in their design. Admittedly, those very large monuments which have been dated – the likes of Durrington Walls or Mount Pleasant – do belong to the latter half of the third millennium, but there are also some very much smaller and broadly contemporary monuments.

Another explanation is to see variation in henge design as the result of regional or local customs. It is easy to pick out basic contrasts between different parts of the British Isles. Single-entrance 'mini-henges' dominate in the Thames Valley, for example, but on the nearby Wessex chalkland the sites are generally much larger, particularly when we consider the four massive 'henge enclosures' of Avebury, Durrington Walls, Marden and Mount Pleasant. Other contrasts are apparent elsewhere, and perhaps the clearest example of a regional tradition is to be found across the central Yorkshire vales between Wakefield and Richmond, where all but two of the eight known henges have an alto-gether distinctive design. With the single exception of Dorchester on Thames, in Oxfordshire, these are the only sites in the British Isles to possess double ditch and bank circuits, along with a pair of entrances, and they are also of a remarkably uniform and large size (**61**), being the biggest off the Wessex chalkland. But the existence of local or regional preferences can only account for some of the variation. It cannot explain why ditch, bank and entrance numbers differ within single regions, or demonstrate why henges in the English Midlands and East Anglia show no clear pattern in either their design or size. And to demonstrate the existence of local or regional traditions is not to explain what this may have meant to the builders and users of the monuments: for to recognise such variation is not necessarily to understand the phenomenon or grasp its ramifications. What is missing is an awareness of how differences in henge design were generated across space and time, and what it meant in terms of social identity.

Some have linked henge variation with the organisation of later Neolithic groups. The arguments are distilled in the chapter's opening quotations, but it is informative to consider Colin Renfrew's (1973) influential account of later Neolithic Wessex. He saw the period as characterised by the development of centralised social groupings, or chiefdoms, where wealth and power was

61 *The central henge and cursus at Thornborough, North Yorkshire.* Photography by Cambridge University Collection of Air Photographs

concentrated in the hands of the few. Living versions of this type of society had been observed in Polynesia and parts of Africa, where there were large communal endeavours like irrigation schemes or the building of monuments. Renfrew considered these to be suitable parallels to the densely populated chalkland of the third millennium and divided the region into distinctive territorial units. He considers the larger henges as centres for the social, religious and economic life of each of these chiefdoms (**62**), and regards the smaller sites as focal points for local ceremonies. Variations in the size of monuments, and the amount of labour invested in their construction, is therefore seen to represent a hierarchy of ceremonial centres across each territorial unit: the

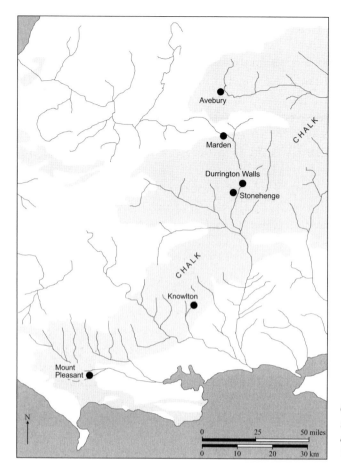

62 *The major henge monuments of the Wessex chalkland.* After Renfrew 1973, fig. 4

smaller monuments were used by individual farming units, with the larger sites acting as regional centres or gathering places for the widespread population of an entire chiefdom. This was perhaps the Neolithic equivalent of the different roles undertaken in more recent times by parish churches and cathedrals, and by town halls and the seat of central government.

Such a hierarchy would certainly account for the huge contrasts in the labour invested in Wessex's later Neolithic monuments. It has been estimated that the giant earthworks at Durrington Walls and Avebury each required about 500,000 man-hours to build using antler picks, ox scapula shovels, baskets and ropes, or what was the equivalent of 250 men working for about a year (Startin & Bradley 1981). This is an impressive commitment, to which we must add the additional labour needed to build their inner features. An estimated 11,000 man-hours may have been expended in the construction of the Southern Circle at Durrington Walls, a calculation which excludes the time it took to fell, trim and transport the timbers. The time taken to locate, move and erect the 247 sarsens within Avebury has not been calculated, but in the reconstruction of the West Kennet Avenue twelve untrained men, under the direction of a foreman and a sub-foreman, raised a relatively small stone in four days (Smith 1965, 218). The mobilisation of such large numbers of people for the construction of both these 'henge enclosures' has been taken by Renfrew and others to indicate the authority of a social élite, and the long periods dedicated to their construction suggests the centralised organisation of a food surplus. They certainly contrast with small sites like the 'mini-henge' of Wyke Down, which could have been built by a couple of families over no more than a day or two.

But Renfrew also makes some shaky assumptions, most notably by linking henges with socio-political organisation. The problems with his approach can be illustrated if we turn our attention to a single region – the vales and uplands of Yorkshire, which, as noted above, produces some of the best evidence for a regional tradition of henge construction. Here we find a series of enclosures, distributed as either widely-spaced single sites or locally clustered to form the densest concentration of henges from across the British Isles (**63**). Their siting may be significant, for whilst it partly reflects the incomplete nature of the archaeological record, it also highlights some meaningful patterns. It is significant, for example, that over half of the known monuments are located along a 7½ mile (12km) stretch of the River Ure. The concentration of six massive henges, near the modern cathedral town of Ripon, clearly testifies to the importance of this particular area during the later Neolithic. But this is perhaps too many closely-spaced sites for each to be interpreted as the central-place of a powerful social grouping, and such an explanation fails to account for the identical size and appearance of these sites. Renfrew's model of later Neolithic society also fails to fit the rest of the region. It is certainly surprising that

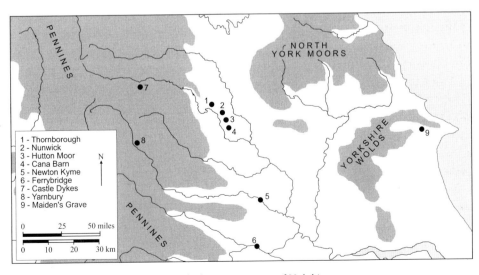

63 *The henge monuments of Yorkshire*

despite the intensity of archaeological fieldwork across the Yorkshire Wolds there is as yet only one definite henge from this area of relatively high population during the later Neolithic, and the eastern edge of the central Pennines, an area which is presumed to have had a lower population, has produced two such sites.

It seems, therefore, that his account of the Wessex chalkland cannot be applied to Yorkshire, and similar problems are evident when other parts of the British Isles are considered, such as to the west of the Pennines, in Cumbria, where the only known henge monuments are the two large enclosures of Mayburgh and King Arthur's Round Table alongside one another near the town of Penrith. The root of the model's shortcomings may be the idea that later Neolithic society was characterised by such centrally controlled and territorially bounded social units as chiefdoms. Such a viewpoint must be at least partly influenced by the present day nation state, but is likely to be wholly inappropriate for the small-scale societies of the British Neolithic, especially those communities occupying areas less densely populated than the Wessex chalkland. Instead of a form of social organisation which placed such great emphasis on fixed notions of group exclusivity and incorporation, it may be more relevant to imagine that there was no absolute criteria for 'belonging' to an individual social group and no constant sense of identity, but a more fluid network of social relationships which changed across both time and space. This alternative view of social organisation moves us away from a single fit-all model, and rather, places the accent on the specific tensions, intentions and motivations of local systems.

The potential value of this approach is demonstrated by returning to the question of how best to understand henge variation. Single sites are frequently of a small size and often appear to have rapidly fallen out of use, or been deliberately backfilled soon after digging, suggesting, as Richard Bradley (1993, 98) has argued, that the act of construction was of more significance than their continued use. It is these smaller henges which are regarded by Renfrew and others as ceremonial foci for local communities, but this actually says little about their exact role and meaning. Their size and short history can be better understood if they are seen as meeting the immediate needs of a community; perhaps they were constructed and used at a time of social crisis, as a means of appealing to the supernatural, or maybe they were centres for seasonal cults. In contrast are the larger henge monuments whose construction involved grand amounts of communal labour, and these tend to cluster together, as with the two sites at Penrith in Cumbria. They may possess a more lengthy history, which could include episodes of maintenance, modification and even transformation, and, as noted, have been regarded as central-places for the reaffirmation of a wider communal identity. But this presupposes the existence of large-scale social unity and an uncomplicated and continuous association between these ceremonial centres and a sense of belonging. Whilst their construction and use probably did involve large-scale participation, this in no way means they must have been the product of a single clan, tribe or chiefdom. They could just as feasibly been the outcome of inter-group festivals, during which people from different socio-political units got together at set times of the year. Or perhaps they resulted from a local cult or supernatural event, as around the 'miracle town' of Lourdes.

What then are the specific tensions, intentions and motivations behind those very much rarer instances where a large henge is directly associated with an earlier ceremonial foci? Examples are few and far between but include some notable monument complexes (**64**). At Dorchester on Thames, in Oxfordshire, the double-ditched henge of Big Rings was built alongside an early Neolithic cursus of impressive length (Whittle *et al.* 1992). Similarly, at the recently excavated Maxey complex, in Cambridgeshire, an ovate-shaped henge, with a narrow ditch and entrance, was actually sited over an earlier cursus monument (Pryor *et al.* 1985). The close spatial relationship between these fourth and third millennium sites certainly differs from the general pattern, mentioned in chapter 1, of henges usually located some distance from cursuses. The distinctiveness of both Dorchester and Maxey is reiterated by the unusual design and

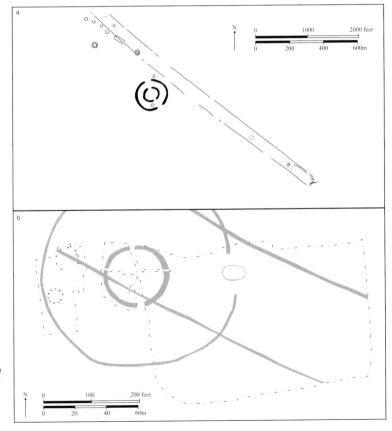

64 *The complexes of a. Dorchester on Thames (after Whittle et al. 1992, fig. 3) and b. Maxey (after Pryor et al. 1985, fig. 40)*

size of each henge, and the cluster of other later Neolithic sites with which they are associated. But how should these characteristics be interpreted? The monuments could be seen as central-places for societies who had achieved long-term stability, and hence a high degree of centralisation, but Richard Bradley (1993, 100-2) has proposed an alternative explanation. He considers the very deliberate siting of these henges as attempts to subvert the meaning of the earlier sites. To him they represent the radical reinterpretation of an established monument complex – and perhaps also the affiliations and relationships between people – rather than any social continuity between the past and the present. In short, the reasons for their siting could have been complex and not necessarily linked with social organisation.

These examples demonstrate how there may have been potentially complex reasons for the design and location of henges. Accordingly, our accounts must move beyond generalised models of society and investigate the specific meanings and roles associated with individual monuments. We must endeavour, in other words, to map out the actual relationships between sites and the tensions, intentions and motivations of local systems. This is difficult given the incompleteness of the available evidence, but it is not impossible. To demonstrate the potential of the approach I wish to return to the henge monuments of Yorkshire. These have been selected not because they are the best studied henges, for if anything the reverse is true. Instead, they constitute an appropriate case study because they are a group of henges about which I know the most, the complex at Thornborough being the focus of my fieldwork. Some are also quite extraordinary monuments, their construction one of the greatest achievements of later Neolithic society. Yet despite this they remain sadly neglected, partly because they are located in the north of England, well away from the areas that have traditionally attracted the interests of prehistorians, but also because they defy our conventional interpretations or models of the third millennium. More than anywhere else, they speak loud and clear of a later Neolithic which differed markedly from place to place, and of henge monuments with contrasting roles.

The Thornborough monument complex

No less than six of Yorkshire's henges are to be found along a 7½ mile (12km) stretch of the River Ure in the low-lying Vale of Mowbray (**65**). This is an unusually dense concentration of monuments, and is all the more remarkable for each site is massive at around 787ft (240m) in diameter, defined by a giant ditch and bank, and interrupted by a pair of opposed entrances (**61**). There is also an outer ditch around each site, which is both irregular and segmentary in outline, and recent excavations have demonstrated that it was probably accompanied by a bank. The henges are most closely sited at Thornborough, where

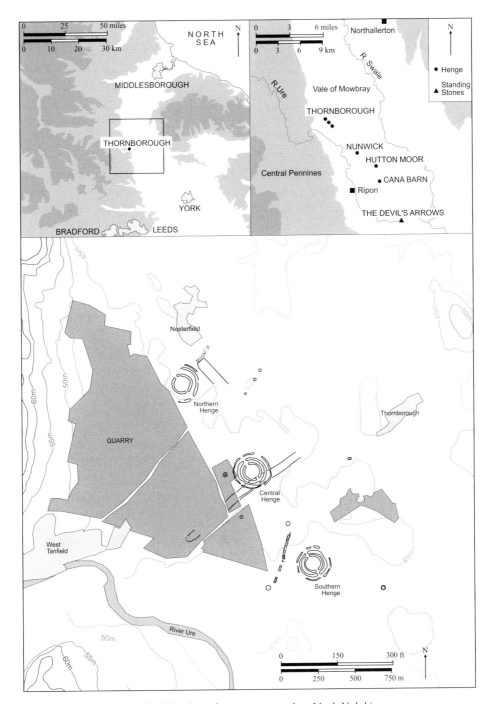

65 *The Thornborough monument complex, North Yorkshire*

an alignment of three equally-spaced and intervisible monuments extend across just under a mile of gravel plateau (Thomas 1955; Harding, J. 2000), a complex whose sheer scale attests to its profound social importance (**65** & **colour plate 15**). Only some 3 miles (5km) downstream, but on exactly the same alignment, is the single henge of Nunwick (Dymond 1964), and the monuments of Hutton Moor and Cana Barn can be found an additional 2 miles (3km) and 3 miles (5km) to the south. The latter two share the same north-south orientation and are located on either side of a low ridge, suggesting that they, like Thornborough, functioned as a single complex.

But how can the distinctive design and closely-spaced location of these monuments be explained? The most obvious feature of the sites is their massive size, suggesting that their construction and use probably involved large-scale participation. Given their shared design and nearness to one another, it also seems likely that there was a unity of purpose behind the construction of all six sites, and the regularity of the Thornborough complex – where the three henges have a shared orientation, an almost identical size and were each spaced approximately 1,800ft (550m) apart – suggests a high degree of planning and organisation. This is in itself quite remarkable and it also seems possible that the ideas and authority which were implicit in their design possessed an unusual chronological longevity. The outer ditch of each monument is segmentary and interrupted in appearance, and as such, differs markedly to the regular and more physically impressive inner ditch and bank. The former appears to have been built as a series of discontinuous sections which varied greatly in size, and such a method of construction is reminiscent of late fourth millennium enclosures like Flagstones or the early third millennium 'formative' henges discussed in chapter 1. Does this therefore suggest that there may be two architectural traditions embedded in the design of these henges? The irregular outer ditches, akin to a tradition of 'formative' henge construction, and the more regular and continuous inner ditches, reflecting an architecture characteristic of many later 'classic' henges.

There is no direct evidence that they did indeed possess two major structural phases, but it certainly seems plausible if we consider the Thornborough complex in greater detail. Here the central henge is superimposed upon an earlier cursus 1½ miles (2.3km) long and 144ft (44m) wide (Vatcher 1960), a form of elongated ceremonial enclosure usually built in the latter half of the fourth millennium. There is nothing coincidental about this siting, for the henge lies at the point where the cursus shifts its course ever so slightly, and the cursus ditch neatly defines the henge's southernmost entrance (**61** & **65**). The reasons for such a deliberate layout are obviously of interest and may suggest the importance of drawing upon and manipulating the power of an earlier monument. But also of concern is how this close siting was practically achieved. It would obviously have been possible if the cursus survived as some form of earthwork, but excavations of the central henge's inner bank during the 1950s demonstrated that the earlier monument was in fact more or less fully silted, and covered with a turf-line by the time of construction (Thomas 1955, 429-31). How then did the builders of the henge know the exact alignment of the cursus, a monument out of use for some centuries? Was it folklore, as the memory of the earlier monument was passed from generation to generation? Did they use distant topographical features or stars to record the alignment of the site? Or was the outer enclosure built earlier than supposed, effectively recording the cursus layout as it still survived as an earthwork? The means by which this spatial juxtaposition was achieved must, at present, remain a mystery, but what is not in doubt is the implied chronological longevity of the complex.

There are other indications that the henges possessed a gradual and elaborate sequence of construction. Small-scale excavation at the southernmost of the Thornborough sites has demonstrated how its outer ditch and bank could have been rebuilt (**66**). The initial earthwork, whilst modest in appearance, was remodelled when the ditch was more or less fully silted. A second and very much narrower ditch was dug into the western side of the original feature and the spoil used to extend the existing bank and close off part of the associated causeway. A narrow and steep-sided slot trench, which could have held some form of fence, was then cut into the inner side of the existing bank. It respects the original causeway and may have been associated with the erection of five timber stakes or small posts across the entranceway.

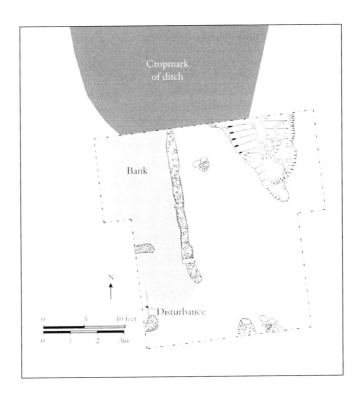

66 *Plan of the excavated outer ditch at the southern Thornborough henge*

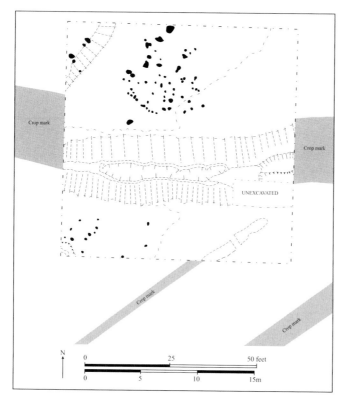

Crop mark

Crop mark

UNEXCAVATED

Crop mark

Crop mark

N

0   25   50 feet

0   5   10   15m

67 *Plan of the excavated outer ditch at the central Thornborough henge*

If this suggests the renewal of the southern henge's outer earthwork then a similar act of restoration has been demonstrated by recent excavations at the outer ditch of the central henge. The feature is far more substantial than that excavated at the southern henge, with a maximum width and depth of 20ft (6m) and 5ft (1.5m) respectively (**67**). Its large size may account for why there was no evidence for rebuilding, but the gravel which should have occurred in its initial fill – representing the natural weathering of the ditch sides immediately after its construction – was absent, suggesting that its flat bottom was cleaned on at least one occasion. What this again indicates is deliberate maintenance over time.

If the henge's inner ditches and banks were a secondary phase of construction, they must have represented a major remodelling of each monument. Their generally continuous inner perimeters served to separate and demarcate an area of sacred space in a way which was not possible with the more modest outer enclosures, constituting a very much more physically impressive barrier. Excavations at both the central and southern Thornborough henges have recorded the inner ditch's width and depth to have been as much as 58ft (17.7m) and 8½ft (2.6m) respectively (**68**). The inner henge banks are as much as 59ft (18m) across and, as discussed in the previous chapter, were probably so high they completely blocked the view across the surrounding landscape (**52**), including the ridge immediately to the west and the more distant Hambleton Hills. The significance attached to the physical enclosure of space is reiterated by the remnants of a banked structure at the excavated inner ditch terminal of the southern Thornborough henge. This badly disturbed feature ran along the side of the causeway and appears to have been associated with a number of timber uprights (**69**). Despite the difficulties in reconstructing its original appearance, there seems little doubt that it served to channel people across the entrance and into the monument, and may have even restricted views into and out of the monument.

The henges at Thornborough could therefore possess an extended history of construction and use. The various acts of rebuilding perhaps illustrate the increasing importance attached to the control of space and the regulation of movement. The alterations made to the outer ditch of the southern henge – the narrowing of the causeway and the erection of a low fence – may show a trend towards the more exclusive enclosure of space which eventually led to the construction of the massive inner ditch and bank. Access to the enclosures was now by just two major entrances, demonstrating the greater physical control of those visiting the sites. But if each of the henges was indeed the product of two major phases of construction, then the remodelling of the complex would have reiterated the importance of the earlier enclosures. These new earthworks were centred within the existing monuments and the orientation of their entrances replicates the major breaks across the outer ditches. There is, in other words, a very deliberate positioning to these subsequent monuments, suggesting that the meanings originally associated with the complex were being extended or embellished within a familiar frame of reference.

68 *The excavated inner ditch terminal of the southern Thornborough henge*

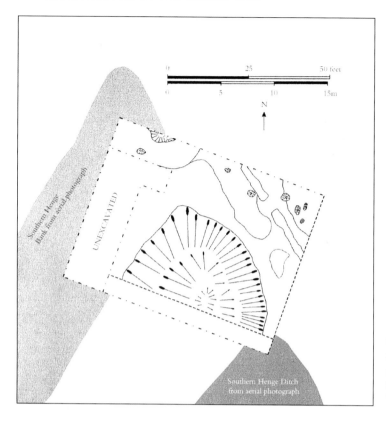

69 *Plan of the excavated inner ditch terminal at the southern Thornborough henge*

Pilgrimage and the sacred river

The chapter began by noting the apparent contradiction between the similarity and variation of henge design. Both characteristics are evident at Thornborough, for here the normal layout of henges was choreographed to create a very distinctive design. The blueprint was then replicated by building three almost identical and regularly spaced monuments. If these are unusual characteristics then the complex is striking in other ways. Unlike large monument concentrations elsewhere, there is no sense in which Thornborough developed by way of chronologically successive sites. It can certainly be contrasted with Dorchester on Thames, in Oxfordshire, and Maxey, in Cambridgeshire, where, as already stated, a henge was similarly associated with an impressively sized cursus (**64**). At both there is a sequence of either spatially or architecturally distinct monuments. The Dorchester cursus was succeeded by a number of 'mini-henges' which respected its main axis, and then by the large henge with its differing orientation (Atkinson *et al.* 1951; Whittle *et al.* 1992). At Maxey, sites of quite different type were superimposed on one another. The cursus and an oval barrow were incorporated into a later henge, with a massive round barrow at its centre, but this monument was in use for a short period of time, then deliberately backfilled, levelled and succeeded by two small pit circles (Pryor *et al.* 1985). At Thornborough, on the other hand, the possible rebuilding of the three enclosures respected their original layout and alignment. There was a unity of purpose which determined both the initial construction and the remodelling of the sites.

To fully appreciate Thornborough's significance it is necessary to consider its general location alongside the River Ure as it descends from Wensleydale into the Vale of Mowbray (**65**). This is of interest when we consider the often stated belief that many henges are near to watercourses because they are participating in later Neolithic lines of communication and movement, and particularly those routeways concerned with the exchange of polished stone axes (**70**), an object known to have been transported over great distances. The argument is especially well made for the Thornborough complex given the likelihood that the known movement of Group VI polished axes – found in large quantities on the Yorkshire Wolds but made of stone from Great Langdale in the Lake District – followed the River Ure as one of the most accessible passages across the central Pennines. Indeed, some of these axes had been deliberately deposited in a boggy area immediately to the north of the complex. The existence of such a potentially important routeway is also illustrated by the other later Neolithic monuments concentrated near to this river as it traverses the low-lying vale. As already mentioned, downstream of Thornborough are the henges of Nunwick, Hutton Moor and Cana Barn, all almost identical in size, design and orientation (**71**). Is it therefore possible that their striking similarities resulted from being located on the same routeway? Thornborough may have been strategically sited along its course, as the River Ure shifts westwards and disappears into the Pennine massif, its southern extent marked by the Devil's Arrows, an alignment

70 *Polished stone axes*

of four or more towering standing stones located just short of the confluence with the River Swale.

The Thornborough complex was therefore well placed to attract a wide range of visitors. It is of interest that the surface lithics collected by fieldwalking indicate that much of the activity across the surrounding landscape took the form of repeated short-term occupancy rather than more permanent settlement. I have already mentioned this evidence in chapter 3, noting how later Neolithic settlement is to be found away from the gravel plateau and its monuments. The largest of the known surface concentrations – on Chapel Hill half a mile to the east of the central henge (**46**) – contains a high proportion of knapping debris, but only small numbers of tools and cores, indicating how groups were only visiting the complex as they undertook various acts of ritual celebration and monumental construction. The same point is made by the light levels of use wear on the worked flint and chert. It also seems likely that the visitors were drawn from a wide spatial catchment. The lithic assemblage is made up of an extensive range of raw materials including those from local gravel sources, chert from the Pennines, and flint from the Yorkshire Wolds and coastline. Such geographical diversity exceeds that of other assemblages from Yorkshire's low-lying vales and was particularly marked during the later Neolithic. Whilst the occurrence of some of this material could well have resulted from the operation of trade networks, the existence of low-grade lithics such as Pennine chert, in an area with abundant amounts of local gravel material, also suggests the influx of distant peoples.

The position of the Thornborough complex on an important routeway, with the evidence for visitors from afar, implies that the monuments were of unusual social significance. One explanation is to see them as a centre for pilgrimage. This would certainly account for Thornborough's distinctive development. Studies of pilgrimage illustrate that the key sites of attraction are places where ritual action and religious belief are most fully played out. It is common for pilgrims to travel to a place separated from the surrounding world, to seek something which lies outside the accustomed patterns of everyday life, a place where heaven and earth intersect. Is it therefore possible that the spatial distinction at Thornborough between the monuments and the surrounding settlements reflects a concern with such a spiritual journey and the notion of rebirth? Furthermore, if Thornborough did indeed serve a transient population of worshippers drawn from across the wider region, then its development may not so readily reflect the ups and downs of local politics as be embedded in more enduring religious priorities – hence, the changelessness of the complex's layout. The importance of pilgrimage could even explain the identical design of those other henges clustered nearby, for there is a tendency for centres of worship on any particular pilgrim route to closely resemble each other.

The River Ure itself must have greatly contributed to the sacredness of the routeway. This is no modest watercourse – as any modern visitor caught during flood time can attest – for it is both wide and powerful (**72**). It has been

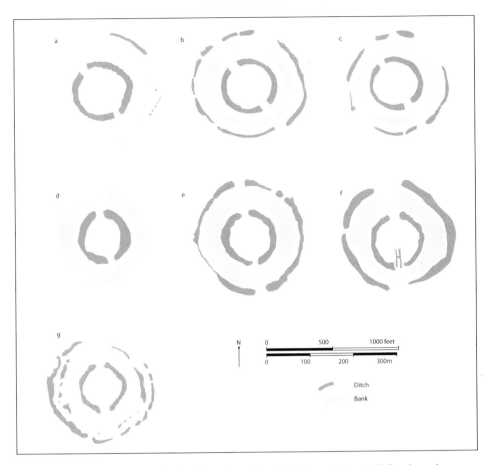

71 *The henge monuments of lowland Yorkshire (a. northern Thornborough, b. central Thornborough, c. southern Thornborough, d. Nunwick, e. Hutton Moor, f. Cana Barn, g. Newton Kyme)*

suggested that the name 'Ure' is derived from the Celtic 'isura' meaning 'holy one', and if later Neolithic religion was indeed obsessed with rivers as symbols of the natural world, as suggested in chapter 2, then here we have a perfect example. On the one hand the river made life possible, providing people with water and a multitude of other vital resources. Its steady course could symbolise both the consistency and continuity of social life. On the other hand the river was uncontrollable, a taker of life. Its fast-flowing current would speak of death and people's inability to escape the inevitable. Consequently, it is not that surprising that henge monuments were built close to its course, or that pilgrims proceeded along its banks, perhaps in an attempt to become spiritually at one with the river's power. These visitors may have even placed polished stone axes or other objects into the murky waters – and two Cumbrian axes have recently been found in a boggy area immediately to the north of the Thornborough complex – echoing a Bronze Age and Iron Age obsession with committing valuable deposits of metalwork to rivers, streams and bogs.

Elsewhere in Yorkshire

It may not, therefore, be appropriate to always consider large henge monuments as the central-places or capitals of centralised social groupings, for some could have had very differing roles. If the cluster of henges alongside the Ure were indeed places of pilgrimage then their significance and renown must have resonated across large expanses of landscape: and if this was the case, it is unsurprising that there is an absence of henges from any immediately adjacent low-lying areas. For aside from the possible site at Catterick, some 9 miles (15km) to the north, the nearest henges are Newton Kyme, nearly 19 miles (30km) to the south, and the even more distant site of Ferrybridge (**63**). Newton Kyme is almost exactly like the sites around Ripon. It possesses a diameter which is identical to these monuments, and its earthworks were probably of similar proportions (**71**). Furthermore, the site consists of an inner ditch and bank, and most unusually, what appears to be traces of two irregular and segmentary outer ditches. Finally, the orientation of its two entrances corresponds with that of Hutton Moor and Cana Barn. Hence, is it possible that Newton Kyme assumed meanings and roles akin to the cluster along the Ure? That it may have also been a pilgrimage centre, serving a large number of social groups, is perhaps demonstrated by its location near to the River Wharfe, a possible routeway for the Group VI axes known to have been moving in large quantities to the Lincolnshire Wolds and Trent Valley.

The impressive size and complexity of these low-lying enclosures contrasts with the small number of other henges known from elsewhere in Yorkshire. The nearest geographically are two sites to the west (**63**), located 12½ miles (20km) apart across the elevated uplands of the central Pennines. Little is known about either of these and their immediate landscapes, but both were of a small size and architecturally straightforward, consisting of a single earthwork perimeter. The largest of the two is Castle Dykes (**73**), near Aysgarth in Wensleydale, with a diameter of some 262ft (80m), but even this is unimpressive when compared to its lowland equivalents. The enclosure's unexcavated ditch and outer bank presently survives to a width of only around 33ft (10m) each and there is a single entrance. The other site is Yarnbury, just over a mile from Grassington in Wharfedale. This poorly-preserved single-entrance site has a diameter of only 116ft (35m) and excavations have demonstrated a rock cut ditch of very modest size, measuring some 8ft (2.5m) across, and a bank of simple dump construction (Dymond 1965).

Their siting, relatively small size, and lack of monumentality suggest that these two henges possessed very different roles from the larger lowland henges. Both Castle Dykes and Yarnbury are situated in the very dales which, as I have already suggested, may have been important routeways across the central Pennines for the movement of stone axes, and it is known that flint was moving in the other direction, from eastern Yorkshire to Cumbria. Yet neither of these

72 *The River Ure, North Yorkshire*

monuments are sited on the dale bottom or sides, but were rather built on the far more elevated fell top plateaux, and as such, were deliberately located away from these very routeways. One can only speculate as to why this was done, but it may represent an attempt to separate these monuments from what could have been perceived as the social pollution created by the comings-and-goings of outsiders, suggesting that their role and meanings were perhaps connected to the secretive rites of local communities. The small size of the monuments hints that they may have been built to meet the immediate needs of the local community. Perhaps they represent the celebration of a specific occasion, or an appeal to the supernatural at a time of social crisis. It is even possible that they were used just once. The overall impression, therefore, is of enclosures whose initial construction was of more significance than any subsequent acts of structural modification and transformation.

The contrast between the low-lying vales and other surrounding areas is also apparent if we consider the East Riding of Yorkshire. This is the most thoroughly researched part of the county and its impressive range of Neolithic and Bronze Age monuments, as well as extensive flint scatters, is well known. Yet it is striking that the only one definite henge known from the area is that of Maiden's Grave (**74**) alongside the Rudston 'D' cursus in the Great Wold Valley. The excavated enclosure is marginally more impressive than Castle Dykes, being some 318ft (97m) across and consisting of a steeply-cut ditch and outer bank, each as much as 38ft (11m) wide, and a pair of opposed entrances (McInnes 1964). There are a number of other possible henges, but all, with the exception of the giant Duggleby Wold enclosure – discussed in

73 *Castle Dykes, North Yorkshire.* Photography by Cambridge University Collection of Air Photographs

chapter 1 (**12**) – and a similarly large and interrupted ditch around another 'Great Barrow' at Wold Newton 284, are also small in size (Stoertz 1997, 30-3). This is certainly surprising when we consider that at least the chalkland wolds, if not other parts of the East Riding, may have supported what would have been very large populations.

Is it therefore possible that henge monuments did not assume a significant role in the later Neolithic of this area, and was the Maiden's Grave henge, and other possibilities, built, as were the two sites in the central Pennines, for specific local occasions? This is all the more likely when we consider the remarkable series of articulated burials under commemorative round barrows from across the East Riding (**9**). They are often associated with a range of highly prestigious artefacts and some date to the later Neolithic. The burials represent a phenomenon which has not been documented for other parts of Yorkshire, and they could have been foci for ceremonial activity during much of the third millennium. But if this was the case then the groups who populated these landscapes must have possessed a more ascribed notion of social identity than was apparent elsewhere. For the burial of individuals under covering round mounds is a means by which the identity or authority of family ancestors can become firmly embedded within society. Their interment would have been acts of conspicuous display, suggesting an emphasis upon the celebration of local consciousness and sentiment. The East Riding can therefore be characterised by communities who had very well defined notions of commonality or affinity, and in such a situation the small number of henges 'belonged' to individual groups, unlike the larger monuments of the lowlands.

In summary, the later Neolithic should in no way be considered as the same across the vales and uplands of Yorkshire. It is possible to recognise important contrasts in both the role of henge monuments and the expression of social identity. On the one hand are the low-lying vales, with their open expanses, long-distance routeways and cluster of truly monumental enclosures. These henges are not associated with the history and mythology of particular communities as their close spacing, sheer size, and identical appearance suggest

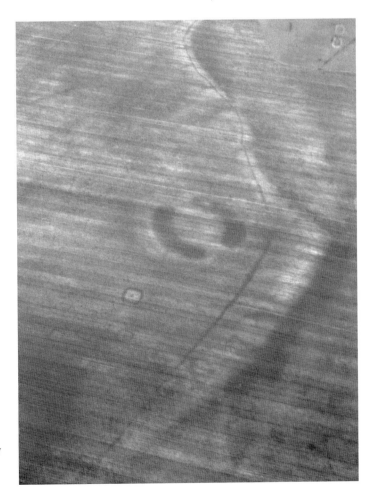

74 *Maiden's Grave, North Yorkshire.* Photography by Cambridge University Collection of Air Photographs

75 *The henges at Penrith, Cumbria. King Arthur's Round Table lies next to the village and Mayburgh's bank is covered in trees.* Crown copyright published by permission of the Ministry of Defence and of the Controller of Her Majesty's Stationery Office

they were rather linked to a sacredness which surpassed such local forms of identity. They were shared by an open and fluid network of social groups, and were consequently places little concerned with emphasising the distinctiveness of individual communities or denying participation to those who may have wished to use the sites. Across the more physically bounded upland landscapes of the dales, wolds and moors, by contrast, group networks were more closed and greater prominence given to the self-conscious expression of within-group solidarity. As a result, the construction and use of monuments, whether it be small henges or round barrows, were expressions of group-based identity and history.

Conclusion

This brief account has hopefully demonstrated that at least in Yorkshire no single model is sufficient to explain the development of the region during the third millennium BC – and it certainly seems unlikely that the henges of the region served as central-places for territorially bound political units, as suggested by Colin Renfrew and others. There was considerable variation in the specific role of the monuments, consequently suggesting that no one definition of later Neolithic religion was accepted by everyone. Instead, the core of ideas and dominant body of symbolism, outlined in the previous chapters, was deployed in different ways, and according to local circumstances, at the grassroots level. Variations in the design of henges were part of overlapping religious traditions, each with their own codes, symbolic nuances and particular rites. This diversity could cover an infinitude of practices and beliefs, but may include life-cycle rituals, rituals of rebellion, initiative rites, rites of office, rites of commemoration, rites of purification, rites of affliction, worship, divination, sacrifice, namings, inaugurations, and so on. The differences in the layout of henge monuments could therefore reflect the specific form of ritual power, spiritual energy or sacredness with which they were associated, indicating the fragmented character of ceremonial life during the third millennium.

Some henge monuments would no doubt be anchored in the history and mythology of particular communities. Those smaller single monuments whose use was often short-lived, for example, could define, communicate, and hence sustain, the particular relationships so essential to group identity. Even some of the larger and more monumental sites, with a history of modification and transformation, may have been places where a sense of political togetherness were created. But there are also those very much rarer sites, as at the Thornborough complex, which were linked to a sacredness more timeless and ahistorical by nature. These can perhaps be described as 'cult centres' to distinguish them from other later Neolithic complexes. They may have attracted a wide range of visitors, or pilgrims, from many different scattered communities and could represent a ritual tradition which spatially surpassed local beliefs and practices. The intentions and motivations implicit to these complexes were clearly different to many other henges. The 'cult centres' created a moral order which was independent of any authoritative power structure. They were shared places where pilgrims attempted to seek out what it was that religion could deliver to them, their families and their social groupings.

The 'cult centres' may have even had far-flung roots. I have already noted two of the three henges clustered around the modern town of Penrith in the Cumbrian lowlands to the east of the Lake District (Topping 1992), located near to one another and between the confluence of two rivers (**75**). There is King Arthur's Round Table, a two-entrance 'classic' site with a wide inner ditch and bank, and the more enigmatic Little Round Table, whose largely levelled remains and badly recorded features make it difficult to confirm as a henge. Alongside is perhaps the most atypical of all British henges, the single-entrance site of Mayburgh, consisting of a huge bank of water-worn cobbles, probably removed from the nearby river, and no ditch. As Aubrey Burl points out, 'in its construction Mayburgh is most closely paralleled by henges in Ireland for whose banks the builders scraped out a shallow scoop around the edge of the interior creating a low domed plateau like an upturned saucer' (2000, 98). He also notes that one of these parallels is at Ballynahatty just to the south-west of Belfast (Hartwell 1998), more or less directly across the Irish Sea from this low-lying Cumbrian vale. This is not to necessarily imagine a site which was built by the Irish, or to evoke an international route of pilgrimage (although this could certainly be a possibility), but rather to see Mayburgh as a deliberate attempt to create a site different or 'exotic' to elsewhere. This would have added attractiveness and mystery to the complex, and the fact that the sites are found along what may have been a crucial riverine routeway, running between the Lake District and the Pennines, suggests that this was also a 'cult centre'. But unlike Thornborough its symbolism evoked a distant land.

The approach outlined in this chapter envisages a later Neolithic society of elaborate, diverse and often overlapping social networks criss-crossing the landscape, each the product of either friendship, ties of blood, of other more formal relations (for example, trading partners or members of cults) between individuals and families. Admittedly this is difficult to visualise, but it helps to liken each network to the individual strands or cord which, when wound together, make up a rope, or in this case, a society. It was a society negotiated at the grass-roots level, rather than imposed from the top down as with the centrally-organised and territorially-based chiefdoms proposed by others. And unlike chiefdoms there was no political 'centre' or 'periphery', no absolute criteria for 'belonging' to an individual social entity, and no constant sense of identity. Instead the picture was more messy, with overlap and variation between and within each network, as well as discontinuity, transformation and fluidity through time. This, then, was a dynamic society, its constituent networks, or strands, sometimes becoming longer and more complex, sometimes becoming shorter or even collapsing, according to locally defined tensions, intentions and motivations. It is only by recreating these networks – and the important roles played by henge monuments in their creation and mutation – that we can hope to populate later Neolithic Britain.

5

THE END OF HENGE MONUMENTS

In overall terms the henge sites and individual burial practices were contem-porary, but the main periods of construction and use of each were not. As the henge and related sites changed and declined in use, the main period of barrow construction and of burials began.

Braithwaite (1984, 98)

The age was deceitful. Seen from a distance it was like the sea, calm and enticing but, closer, eddies and waves and tidal-races were visible in society. Nothing was still. People changed. There were conflicts and alliances, inven-tions and archaisms, sudden movements and years of stagnation. Life, like a creeping vine, retained its roots, but its growing tendrils twisted and turned, spread wide, overshadowed the lower, older leaves.

Burl (1987, 150)

The late third millennium

The archaeological record testifies to over 500 years of 'classic' henge building and the tradition's decline towards the end of the third millennium BC. The small number of radiocarbon dates tell us that most of the dated earthworks were built before 2200 BC, although the Devil's Quoits, in Oxfordshire, and the southern Thornborough henge, in North Yorkshire, have produced later dates from their lower ditch fills (**6** & **Table 1**). The first of these is 2140-1740 BC, but cannot be accepted as determining the construction of the Devil's Quoits henge given a very much earlier primary date of 2900-2200 BC and third millennium dates from its secondary fill (Barclay *et al.* 1995, 45-6). There is also good reason for ignoring the very late date of 1750-1510 BC from

Thornborough. It was from a small charcoal fragment which could have quite easily percolated into the top of the primary fill from a higher level, and the ditch bottom was perhaps cleaned out, making its deposits very much later than its initial construction. Disregarding these two determinations means that no henge has produced a date range from its primary contexts which falls exclusively in the second millennium, suggesting a relatively clear-cut end, at least in terms of radiocarbon chronology, to their construction. But how did this come to pass and was it connected to a wider process of deep-rooted change?

The last few centuries of the third millennium are usually characterised in the archaeological literature by a major transition. If the first henge monuments marked the beginning of the later Neolithic, then their decline, and final abandonment, is seen as bringing the period to a close, and ushering in the next phase of British prehistory, the *early Bronze Age*. The name of the new period suggests a major technological advance, and indeed, copper and gold were used for the manufacture of small daggers and personal ornaments like pins. However, metalwork remained uncommon for many centuries and the early Bronze Age is better known for a new set of ritual beliefs and practices, typified in the archaeological record by the 'single-grave tradition', or burial of articulated inhumations, often with grave-goods, under covering round barrows (**76 & 77**). There was nothing new about this practice for its origins lie in the fourth millennium (see chapter 1), but what was now different was the extent to which it was practised. The numbers of these burials start to increase from around 2200 BC and by the close of the millennium they are found

76 *An early Bronze Age single-grave burial at Raunds, Northamptonshire.* Copyright Northamptonshire County Council

77 *An early Bronze
Age round barrow*

throughout the British Isles. The synchronicity between their appearance and
the waning popularity of henges – alluded to in this chapter's opening
quotation – suggests a fundamental reworking of society. If the henge
monuments were connected to communal-based ritual, in which the needs
and aspirations of the group were emphasised over any one person, then the
single-grave tradition was all about the individual, with grave-goods used to
signify their rank or status (Braithwaite 1984; Shennan 1982; Thorpe &
Richards 1984). The last few centuries of the third millennium therefore saw
the replacement of one type of society by another.

  This process of change is regarded as having its roots in the later Neolithic
and its range of wonderfully crafted items. The traditional henge-based system
– or what has been described as a 'ritual authority structure' – relied on the
mobilisation of labour for the construction of these monuments, and its success
must have ultimately rested on the belief that such efforts were in society's best
interests. The commonality and longevity of henge construction points to the
achievements of the 'ritual authority structure', but this is not to say it was
always smooth-running. It would only be human nature for arguments and
disagreements to have occurred, resulting perhaps in long-term grievances
between families and groups. There could have been those who were disillu-
sioned with the system and even perhaps a growing separation between a
priestly élite concerned with co-ordinating ritual and commoners who turned
to alternative forms of expression. The chief alternative during the later
Neolithic was what anthropologists call a 'prestige goods economy', or the
acquisition of high-status objects (such as finely-made flint axes and knives, boar
tusks, bone pins and jet belt-sliders) for the expression of power, especially at
the graveside (**9**). These two systems were dependent on contradictory beliefs
and practices, so they clashed and competed: a process colourfully likened by

Aubrey Burl in the second of the chapter's opening quotations to 'eddies and waves and tidal-races'. By the close of the third millennium there was one clear winner. The 'prestige goods economy', with its emphasis on inequality, competition and symbols of power, was now the dominant form of political authority.

The success of the one system over the other is seen to have depended greatly on events across the English Channel. In the Netherlands and the lower Rhine, from about 2500 BC, there developed a range of finely-crafted objects of which the most common was a distinctive form of highly decorated pottery vessel, or *Beaker*, from which the other items – namely copper daggers, rectangular stone wristguards (presumably worn to protect the archer from the backlash of a bowstring), distinctive barbed-and-tanged arrowheads, stone axe hammers, and a range of personal ornaments like V-perforated jet or shale buttons – took their name. This Beaker package spread rapidly and widely throughout central and western Europe in the latter half of the third millennium, eventually appearing across eastern Britain in the region's single-grave burials. They were unlike the traditional material culture of the later Neolithic, the Beaker's form and decoration being quite at odds with more crudely-made indigenous pots, and the other objects were also without parallel (**78** & **79**). Their exoticness and newness must have been a powerful weapon in the clash between the 'ritual authority structure' and the 'prestige goods economy', providing a great deal of status to anyone lucky enough to acquire the objects. As a result, more and more people tried to benefit from the items and they quickly became popular. The old ways attempted to fight back, by building some of the larger henge monuments, but this only served to reinforce social division. The 'ritual authority structure' was too rigid a system, lacking the flexibility to respond to the new political realities, and by about 2100 BC, the Beaker package had brought about the total dislocation and collapse of traditional society.

There is much to recommend this interpretation of the late third millennium. It is sociologically sensitive in that it envisages later Neolithic society as dynamic, rather than unchanging, as suffering from its own tensions and divisions, instead of being a prehistoric utopia, and as open to external influences or winds of change. However, we can also question the interpretation's broad thrust. The Beaker package is, in truth, rather poorly dated, but its first appearance in the British Isles is now thought to have been as early as 2600 BC (Kinnes *et al.* 1991), with it not becoming widely adopted for at least another four hundred years, at about the same time that henge construction ends. This means a chronologically lengthy co-existence between Beakers and henges, yet the above storyline takes no account of the links or relationships which must have developed between the two over such a long timespan. It may especially be simplistic to imagine a neatly definable period during which the 'ritual authority structure' gave way to the 'prestige goods economy'. The implausibility of a single horizon of change, in which one system was replaced by another, is borne out by the likelihood that henges were in use for greatly

78 *Beaker grave-goods from a primary burial at Raunds, Northamptonshire.* Copyright English Heritage

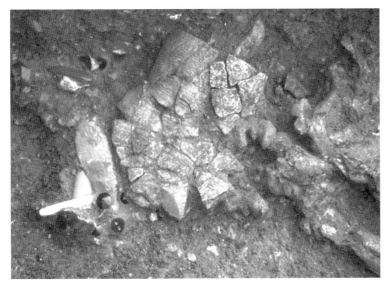

79 *Detail of Beaker grave-goods from the feet of a primary burial at Raunds, Northamptonshire.* Copyright English Heritage

varying lengths of time, some even continuing to be used early in the second millennium. The radiocarbon evidence may suggest that no new monuments were built after approximately 2200 BC, but this is not to say there was a distinct phase of abandonment, for in reality they were falling out of use over an extremely long period of time, in response, perhaps, to the constantly changing circumstances of those who built and used the sites.

It is also possible to question whether there were two competing systems. Previous chapters have argued that henge monuments were associated with a distinctive set of beliefs and practices, but can the same be said of the 'prestige goods economy'? Essential to its existence is the idea that some objects were symbols of power or prestige, used, most notably, as grave-goods. There is no doubting that these items were finely-crafted and often elaborate, their manufacture requiring a great deal of expertise. But as Thomas (1996, chapter 6) has recently questioned, this does not necessarily mean they were prestigious or special. Many of the objects used as grave-goods were in fact more common than would be expected if they were symbols of power, and found in contexts other than burials, such as the large quantities of well-made arrowheads, stone maceheads and polished flint knives collected during fieldwalking across the Yorkshire Wolds. Their acquisition, use and deposition may have therefore communicated things other than status or rank. Recent accounts even dispute that Beakers were ever inherently special or prestigious (Case 1995; Boast 1995), noting their common occurrence on settlements, and the fact that many of these were of higher quality than those in single-graves. These studies challenge the view that a 'prestige goods economy' ever existed as an independent socio-political reality, or indeed, that the final Neolithic can be characterised by its increasing popularity and its replacement of traditional society. But given this, *how* can we understand the latter half of the third millennium and why the henge phenomenon came to an end?

Cults of the dead

The one factor which distinguishes the early Bronze Age from the final Neolithic is the widespread popularity of the single-grave tradition. This burial practice is regarded as an intrinsic part of the 'prestige goods economy', and as such, opposed to the 'ritual authority structure' and its henges. But this was a tradition with a long history, appearing, as noted in chapter 1, over a thousand years before in the early Neolithic. The earliest examples are found across Yorkshire's East Riding and the Peak District, consisting of small numbers of complete skeletons buried under a round mound and accompanied by a rich array of objects (**9** & **80**). A scattered distribution of Neolithic round barrows and ring ditches (some of which are ploughed-out examples of the former), is also known from central Scotland, north-east England, the English midlands, East Anglia and the Thames Valley. Some of these have been found with individual interments and grave-goods. The limited dating evidence points towards their construction in either the later fourth millennium or the early third millennium. The single burial tradition is particularly well represented in the upper Thames Valley, where it was associated with a wide range of monuments, including a late form of long barrow characterised by its short oval mound and surrounding ditch (**19**). The latter are also known from Wessex, first appearing in the fourth millennium, probably centuries before the earliest Neolithic round barrows from the chalkland. This link with a variant of the traditional form of burial monument suggests a conscious attempt to connect the new with the old. These southern communities may have been less amenable to change and it is likely that the first round barrows occurred some time after their introduction elsewhere.

These monuments represent a radical departure from the social collectivity celebrated at many of the earlier long barrows. Whilst not exclusively associated with the rite of single burial – cremations, disarticulated remains, or no human bone at all are also found – many possess a central 'primary' grave of either one, two or three complete individuals. They suggest that a particular dead person, and their identity or life history, was now the focus of mortuary practice and everything else done at the sites. The burial of a fleshed corpse, and the subsequent construction of a covering mound or the digging-out of a surrounding ditch, fixed the person's story in both space and time, creating what John Barrett (1994, 115) has described as an 'image of death'. Placing objects in the grave would also have been part of the process, their insertion creating a narrative or story about the buried individual, and indeed, the mourners actually placing the objects. All this suggests that the early Neolithic system of communal ancestry – best represented by the fragmentary skeletal deposits commonly found with the earlier long barrows – was being complemented, if not partially replaced, by one whereby specific individuals were glorified after their death. Their ego now became part of the stories that living peoples told about themselves and their families, suggesting a concern with genealogy, whereby groups traced their roots through named individuals rather than to an anonymous body of ancestors. It must surely be of interest that the majority of primary burials were of adult males.

The human bone deposited at many henge monuments is likely to have meant something completely different, for here complete or nearly complete skeletons are rare. The largest human bone assemblage has been found on the 'formative' henge of Stonehenge, Wiltshire, dating to the first half of the third millennium (Cleal et al. 1995b). The majority were cremations – over fifty being found in the Aubrey Holes and the ditch fill – although scattered and fragmentary unburnt bone was also found (**50d**). The nature of these remains is paralleled at other sites which date to the first half of the third millennium: at Llandegai A, where cremated bone was found in the ditch fill of a segmentary circular enclosure just outside the henge's entrance and surrounding a small pit with the remains of a child (Houlder 1968); at the four Dorchester on Thames 'mini-henges' in Oxfordshire (**20**), each with between 21 and 49 cremations from their interiors, upper ditch fills, and from just outside their ditches (Atkinson et al. 1951; Whittle et al. 1992, 153-8); and at the 'mini-henge' of Wyke Down, Dorset, where small amounts of cremated bone and human skull fragments had been deliberately placed into three of the recuts dug into the site's circuit of twenty-six pits (Bradley et al. 1991, 96, fig. 3.22). All these deposits contrast with the 'primary' burials of Neolithic round barrows or ring ditches in that individual identity and status has been deliberately destroyed, largely

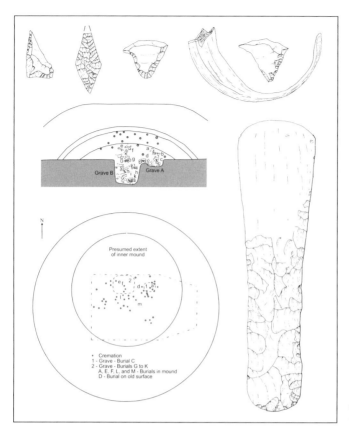

80 *The Duggleby Howe 'Great Barrow', East Yorkshire, and some of its grave-goods.* After Mortimer 1905

through the act of burning the human remains. The emphasis, in other words, was upon the celebration and commemoration of one's anonymous ancestors, and although Llandegai A did produce a central deposit which 'may have special meaning' (Houlder 1968, 218), it was of a child. The latter's young age may have negated the likelihood that it possessed an individual identity, explaining why children are rarely found as 'primary' single-grave burials without an accompanying adult (Kinnes 1979, fig. 1.1-4).

Unburnt human bone is much more common on henges built during the middle or later third millennium. Their role or significance may have again been very different to the articulated burials of the Neolithic round barrows and ring ditches. They are usually found in a disarticulated state, and when complete or nearly complete skeletons do occur, they are of children or deposited after the site's initial construction, during the currency of Beaker pottery or later. One of the largest assemblages is from Avebury, Wiltshire, where extensive sections of the enclosure's giant ditch have been excavated. A total of fourteen separate findspots of fragmentary human bone were found, the vast majority from skulls, mandibles and long bones, along with a female inhumation which is described below (Gray 1934, 146-8). Broadly similar in both its quantity and nature were the two infant burials and fragmentary skull remains from the secondary filling of the ditch terminals flanking the northern entrance of Mount Pleasant, Dorset (Wainwright 1979, 42-5, plates XXIVa-b). Much smaller amounts of human bone are known from elsewhere. Skull and long bone fragments were found at Woodhenge, Wiltshire, along with a cremation, the skeleton of a young adult male from the bottom of its ditch, and an infant from a grave at the site's centre (Pollard 1995, 145, 149-50). At least six skull fragments were high in the fills of two of the remarkably deep shafts at Maumbury Rings, Dorset (Bradley 1976, 26-7), and there were four skull and long bone fragments at Durrington Walls (Wainwright 1971, 191). The fact that the majority of these deposits were disarticulated suggests that ancestral worship dominated the use and significance of human bone at henge monuments, and the high proportion of skull fragments could indicate how the head, as opposed to other body parts, was the ultimate symbol of these spiritual beings.

Some accounts have gone further in linking the famous henge monuments of the Wessex chalkland with death and the afterlife (Parker Pearson & Ramilisonina 1998; Pitts 2000, 258ff; Whittle 1997). Taking their prompt from the anthropological observation that stone's hardness and durability makes it the perfect medium for symbolising ancestry, these studies have reconsidered the pairing of henges with either stone or wooden circles. Across the eastern Salisbury Plain there is Stonehenge, whose magnificent stone circles have already been discussed, and the nearby sites of Durrington Walls and Woodhenge, with their equally impressive timber structures and evidence for communal feasting. Each of these henges is seen as part of a complex ceremonial landscape. The latter two were places where the living congregated with the newly dead, whilst Stonehenge – with its standing stones and large number of cremations – was the final destination for the dead, home to the ancestors and from time to time those who wished to communicate with them. A similar interpretation was proposed for Avebury and the contemporary timber structures located over a mile away at the Sanctuary – where concentric circles of large wooden uprights very similar to those at Woodhenge and Durrington Walls, but without an encircling bank and ditch, were built – and the recently discovered complex of massive circular palisades at West Kennet. Here, as across the eastern Salisbury Plain, the timber and stone circles were the starting point and final destination on the 'all-important journey from the world of the living to that of the ancestors' (Pitts 2000, 272). If correct, it reiterates the contrast between the mortuary rites undertaken at the henges and at other broadly contemporary monuments like round barrows and ring ditches.

These observations highlight what might have been two very different ideologies. On the one hand were the henges, representing what could be described as later Neolithic mainstream religion. The deposition of human bone played only a minor role in the communal rituals enacted within these monuments, but where it does occur it shows a concern with commemorating an anonymous body of ancestral spirits, in a way which is very reminiscent of fourth millennium beliefs and practices. The pre-Beaker single-grave tradition was very different, concerned as it was with deliberately perpetuating the individual ego after death – a contrast which is reiterated by round barrows and ring ditches being sited away from henges, or where this was not the case, being earlier in date than the nearby henge. The largest known number of these burials is from across Yorkshire's East Riding, where there were few henge monuments (see chapter 4). Here, the tradition culminated in the building of six known 'Great Barrows', probably during the early third millennium. The best known of these is Duggleby Howe, its massive mound associated with an unusually large number of inhumations, placed in a shaft-grave with an extremely rich array of grave-goods, and over fifty cremations (**80**). The upper Thames Valley has much smaller numbers of Neolithic single-graves. At Stanton Harcourt, near Oxford, at least four broadly contemporary ring ditches – one with a female burial and grave-goods of either a late fourth or early third millennium date – were just half a mile or less from the Devil's Quoits henge (Barclay *et al.* 1999, chapter 5), but crucially, the latter was probably built some time after the other monuments.

The fourth millennium origin of the single-grave tradition, and its presence in areas where there were few or no henge monuments, suggest how it may have been *independent* of the religious ideas and practices which dominated the later Neolithic. This is not to repeat those arguments made elsewhere, and summarised in this chapter's introduction, which proposed two mutually antagonistic and competing ideologies – one egalitarian, one ranked – or what are described as the 'ritual authority structure' and the 'prestige goods economy'. These surely over-simplify the socio-political realities of the time by seeing communities as subscribing exclusively to one or the other. Can we really expect that the building of sites like Avebury or Durrington Walls, for example, did not result in a complex set of new relationships, out of which some individuals or groups emerged with influence? Would they really have not resulted in some groups acquiring greater material wealth, esoteric knowledge and social power than others? The answer must surely be 'no', for the construction, and indeed use, of at least the larger sites required the co-ordination of both people and resources, circumstances from which some would proffer. Or as John Barrett (1994, 105) puts it, these henges 'contributed towards the construction of a ritual élite who, at certain moments, may have spoken and acted on behalf of the wider community. Whatever their original, and continuing, claim to assert this authority – be it age, gender, lineage – that authority was transformed by their involvement in these increasingly elaborate practices. A new form of person was created in this way, one who perhaps belonged to an increasingly remote and sacred community and who, through forms of dress and through the food and drink consumed at moments of ritual display, may have emphasised their proximity to the gods or the ancestors or to other forms of esoteric knowledge'. Henges would have therefore given rise to leaders, even long-term social inequality, and so the contrasts between the 'ritual authority structure' and the 'prestige goods economy' seem less meaningful, or indeed, the categories themselves less relevant.

We can conclude from this that the henge builders, and not just those peoples burying their dead under round mounds or within ring ditches, may have sometimes adopted ideas, practices and objects by which to express their newly-found identities. If the henges were part of an over-arching set of religious beliefs and practices, then the single-grave tradition can be understood as a strategy employed at a grass-roots level to meet specific needs, perhaps as a cult whose popularity waxed and waned according to local circumstances. It was originally adopted by communities in the late fourth or early third millennium, but as time passed the efforts of at least some became increasingly dedicated to the building and using of henges, in turn resulting in new forms of social identity and inequality. This may well explain why the cult reappears in the latter half of the third millennium, this time associated with henges. At the centuries old site of Stonehenge, the skeleton of an adult male was found in the upper ditch silts with three arrowheads and radiocarbon dated to 2400-2140 BC (Allen & Bayliss 1995, 532-3; McKinley 1995, 456). In the secondary fill of the ditch terminal opposite Avebury's southern entrance was the 'dwarf' burial, so-called because the female skeleton was diminutive in size (Gray 1934, 145-6). It is dated by an underlying deposit of charcoal to 2450-1830 BC (Pitts & Whittle 1992, table 1). Skeletons were also found at the foot of four of the orthostats along Avebury's West Kennet Avenue, with more fragmentary remains beside two others and from two of the enclosure's inner stone-holes (Smith 1965, 204, 209-10, 230-1). In the relatively late henge of Gorsey Bigbury, Somerset, a cist burial was found in the ditch bottom, containing parts of at least two adults in association with grave-goods (Harding & Lee 1987, 261), and at Woodhenge an unaccompanied young adult male placed in a shallow grave cut into the ditch base is thought to be broadly contemporary with the site's construction between 2410-1970 BC (Pollard 1995, 145).

The objects of the Beaker package seem to be closely linked to this phenomenon's reappearance. Three barbed and tanged arrowheads, or what are Beaker-style items, accompanied the skeleton in the Stonehenge ditch; a Beaker sherd, barbed and tanged arrowhead, flint knife and five bone objects were placed in the cist at Gorsey Bigbury; and two of the graves along the West Kennet Avenue were found with possibly early Beaker pots. This style of pottery is also found throughout the ditch fills of a number of henge monuments. Radiocarbon dates from these contexts span the later third millennium and first few centuries of the second millennium, but could be as early as between 2500 to 2200 BC at some henges (Kinnes et al. 1991, appendix 1b). The implication is that its deposition was occurring during the main currency of these monuments, and in some cases, not that long after their initial construction, maybe as some people became more powerful than others. It is interesting to note that Beakers have been likened to a drinking vessel on account of their shape and size, even as part of a cult which involved the consumption of alcohol (Burgess 1980; Sherratt 1997). There is little direct evidence for seeing them as exclusively associated with alcoholic beverages, but every chance that they were part of some new eating and drinking etiquette, perhaps adopted by the nouveau riche of the later third millennium. The pots could have been everyday ware for those individuals and families who had decided to use a distinctive form of object to categorise themselves as different, or conceivably better, than others. Alternatively, they could have been integral to a new feasting ritual, performed at certain times and at certain places, including at henges. This is, after all, a role with which Grooved Ware has been connected, and the fact that many Beakers are smaller than these vessels suggests that feasting had perhaps become a more exclusive activity.

What is important here is the link between Beakers and henges. The pottery is certainly not found on every enclosure, but it is common enough to suggest that whatever it represented it was doing so at henges when they were still very much in vogue. Its adoption was not therefore the result of a major upheaval, as one society gave way to another, and despite being closely associated with the re-emerging cult of single burial, it is found on henges which continued to serve as important ritual foci. Nowhere is this better represented than at Stonehenge, where a small number of Beaker sherds were associated with the site's long sequence of stone settings (**59**), spanning some eight hundred years during the later third and early second millennium (Cleal 1995c). It was suggested that the pottery's deposition was in fact 'a very minimal part of the monument's history, and perhaps more or less incidental . . . when so little of that ceramic and none of the artefacts traditionally associated with it were found there' (Cleal 1995d, 356). The lack of any great transformation is even evident where it is possible to link Beakers with the major rebuilding of a henge in the later third millennium, perhaps as the beneficiaries of the original monument

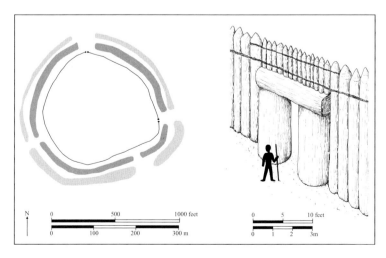

81 *The palisade at Mount Pleasant, Dorset, and a reconstruction of its eastern entrance.* After Wainwright 1979, figs 98 & 100

developed new ways of expressing themselves. At the enclosure of Mount Pleasant, the pottery is directly linked with either the erection or destruction of sarsen uprights, including a central 'cove-like' structure, on the site of its inner timber structure (**57**), and also with the building of a giant palisade, which stood to a height of 20ft (6m) or more (**81**), around the inside of the older earthwork (Wainwright 1979, 28-31, 48-68). The palisade would have required the cutting down, preparation and erection of over 1,600 massive posts of oak, representing a major investment of both energy and time. Both events at Mount Pleasant have been radiocarbon dated to the very late third millennium, and in each instance they represent the elaboration of what already existed, as opposed to the creation of something new and very different.

The new strategies which emerged towards the end of the later Neolithic also included additions to the landscapes around henge monuments. At least two Beaker burials were deposited, under covering round barrows, along Stonehenge's near north-western horizon less than a mile away (Cleal & Allen 1995a, 488-9; 1995b figs 22-3), a link which is all the more apparent when we consider the bluestone fragments found with one of these. A particularly dense concentration of earlier Beaker graves has been found in the Stanton Harcourt area of the upper Thames Valley (Barclay *et al.* 1995, chapters 5-6), within a mile or so to the north-west of the Devil's Quoits henge. This included five burials in 'flat' graves and another two in small ring ditches, neither of which are likely to have been covered by mounds. The long-term remembrance of places associated with an earlier manifestation of the single-grave cult is demonstrated by the siting of one of these burials on a centuries old Neolithic double-ring ditch with a central female grave. This closely-knit landscape of a henge and Neolithic or Beaker burial monuments is a remarkable expression of the ebb and flow of religious trends and local fortunes. Both these archaeologically rich, and relatively well researched landscapes, are far from typical of the situation around every henge, but they nevertheless demonstrate a tendency on the part of these enclosures to act as magnets for the single-grave cult. Glimpses of the process are evident elsewhere, such as a mile to the west of Mount Pleasant, where a line of barrows were sited along a ridge, one covering a late third millennium burial (Smith *et al.* 1997).

The Beaker burials were not therefore the physical manifestation of a completely different form of society, as has been argued elsewhere, but an expression of slowly emerging local relationships, rivalries and forms of expression. They tell of a gradual renegotiation rather than rapid transformation during the late third millenium and early second millennium. These new monuments created alternative foci for ritual life, and through time the henges themselves, and all they represented, became distant or irrelevant – or as John Barrett (1994, 111) puts it, 'the henges could have become unintelligible, irrelevant or have been more directly challenged by knowledges and truths built out of an engagement with different symbolic resources'. The earlier round

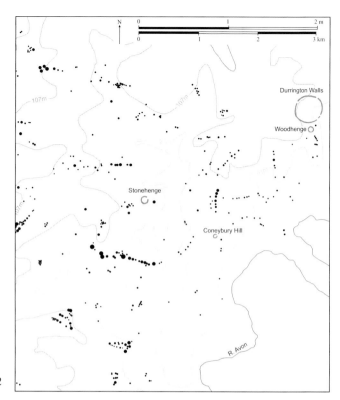

82 *The round barrows and ring ditches of the eastern Salisbury Plain, Wiltshire. After RCHME 1979, map 2*

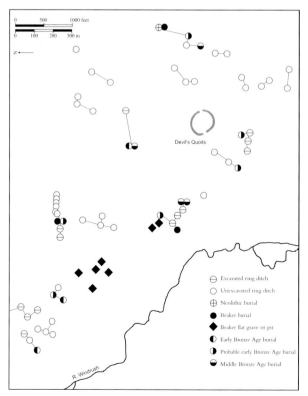

83 *The round barrows and ring ditches of Stanton Harcourt, Oxfordshire. After Woodward 2000, fig. 50*

barrows were now points of convergence, or 'founder' monuments, for other new burials and mounds, and by the early second millennium *cemeteries* – or what are regarded as the dynastic burial ground of families or groups – had emerged in and around many henges, collectively forming dense clusters of burial sites. The two early sites built immediately to the north-west of Stonehenge developed into a cemetery of about fifteen barrows, and at the same time, a large number of other cemeteries were raised across the surrounding landscape (**82**), their distinctive mounds stretching across and dominating the surrounding ridges. As many as sixteen closely-sited cemeteries, each of between two and seven round barrows or ring ditches, had sprung up around the earlier burials at Stanton Harcourt (**83**), creating new centres of worship near the henge of Devil's Quoits. These examples, and many more besides, attest to an inversion of religious belief in the final Neolithic and early Bronze Age. Sacredness, which was once contained and protected by the henge earthworks, had been set free as people built temples to themselves. Its spirits and gods had returned to the landscape from which they originally came.

Conclusion

At the beginning of this book, I argued that the origins of the later Neolithic lie in a couple of hundred years of crisis and social invention culminating in a religious 'revolution'. The end of this period, and the beginning of the early Bronze Age, is a very different story. There was no tear in history, or major horizon of change, as the old spirits and gods were swept away by a tidal wave of change. Instead the gradual renegotiation of socio-political realities at the grass-roots level gave rise to a new way of doing things, in which the arcane religion of the later Neolithic was marginalised by a more easily accessible set of family-based beliefs. Barrow cemeteries became places where the histories and personal inter-relationships of individuals and closely-knit social groups were embedded in the landscape – in short, they were monumental expressions of *genealogy*. But despite the shift in beliefs, henges continued to be a part of people's consciousness, acting as historical anchors, or points of legitimisation, for the sprawling barrow cemeteries. They were built by the descendants, real or otherwise, of those buried in the barrows, and this, of course, is the reason why the latter are found in the general vicinity of these enclosures, for it allowed the builders and users of the burial monuments to acknowledge their own descent. In such a way, the henge phenomenon slipped quietly and effortlessly into the new world order of the Bronze Age.

BIBLIOGRAPHY

Allen, M.J. & Bayliss, A. 1995. 'Appendix 2: the radiocarbon dating programme.' In R.M.J. Cleal *et al.*, *Stonehenge in its Landscape: Twentieth-century Excavations.* London: English Heritage Archaeological Report 10, 511–35

Atkinson, R.J.C., Piggott, C.M. & Sandars, N.K. 1951. *Excavations at Dorchester, Oxon.* Oxford: Ashmolean Museum

Baillie, M.G.L. & Brown, D.M. 1995. *A Slice Through Time: Dendrochronology and Precision Dating.* London: B.T. Batsford Ltd

Baillie, M.G.L. 2002. 'Oak dendrochronology: some recent archaeological developments from an Irish perspective.' *Antiquity* 76(292), 497–505

Barclay, A. & Halpin, C. 1999. *Excavations at Barrow Hills, Radley, Oxfordshire. Volume I: The Neolithic and Bronze Age Monument Complex.* Oxford: Oxford Archaeological Unit (Thames Valley Landscapes Volume 11)

Barclay, A., Gray, M. & Lambrick, G. 1995. *Excavations at the Devil's Quoits, Stanton Harcourt, Oxfordshire, 1972-3 and 1988.* Oxford: Oxford Archaeological Unit (Thames Valley Landscapes: the Windrush Valley Volume 3)

Barclay, G.J. 1983. 'Sites of the third millennium BC to the first millennium AD at North Mains, Strathallan, Perthshire.' *Proceedings of the Society of Antiquaries of Scotland* 113, 122–281

Barclay, G.J. & Russell-White, C.J. 1993. 'Excavations in the ceremonial complex of the fourth to second millennium BC at Balfarg/Balbirnie, Glenrothes, Fife.' *Proceedings of the Society of Antiquaries of Scotland* 123, 43–210

Barnatt, J. 1989. *Stone Circles of Britain: Taxonomic and Distributional Analysis and a Catalogue of Sites in England, Scotland and Wales.* Oxford: British Archaeological Reports (British Series) 215i & ii

Barnatt, J. 1990. *The Henges, Stone Circles and Ring Cairns of the Peak District.* Sheffield: University of Sheffield Archaeological Monograph 1

Barrett, J.C. 1984. *Fragments from Antiquity. An Archaeology of Social Life in Britain, 2900-1200 BC.* Oxford: Blackwell

Boast, R. 1995. 'Fine pots, pure pots, Beaker pots.' In I. Kinnes & G. Varndell (eds), *'Unbaked Urns of Rudely Shape': Essays on British and Irish Pottery.* Oxford: Oxbow Monograph 55, 69–80

Bradley, R. 1976 'Maumbury Rings, Dorchester: the excavations of 1908-1913.' Reprinted from *Archaeologia* 105, 1-97

Bradley, R. 1993. *Altering the Earth.* Edinburgh: Society of Antiquaries of Scotland

Bradley, R. 1998. *The Significance of Monuments: on the Shaping of Human Experience in Neolithic and Bronze Age Europe.* London and New York: Routledge

Bradley R. & Thomas, J. 1984. 'Some new information on the henge monument at Maumbury Rings, Dorchester.' *Proceedings of the Dorset Natural History and Archaeology Society* 106, 132-4

Bradley, R., Brown, A., Cleal, R., Green, M., & Legge, A.J. 1991. 'Henge monuments: the excavations on Wyke Down. The excavated material and its distribution.' In J.C. Barrett *et al.*, *Landscape, Monuments and Society: the Prehistory of Cranborne Chase.* Cambridge: University Press

Braithwaite, M. 1984. 'Ritual and prestige in the prehistory of Wessex *c.*2000-1400 BC: a new dimension to the archaeological evidence.' In D. Miller & C. Tilley (eds), *Ideology, Power and Prehistory.* Cambridge: University Press, 93–110

Brewster, A. 1984. *The Excavation of Whitegrounds, Burythorpe.* Wintringham: John Gett

Burgess, C. & Shennan, S. 1976. 'The Beaker phenomenon: some suggestions.' In C. Burgess & R. Miket (eds), *Settlement and Economy in the Third and Second Millennium BC*. Oxford: British Archaeological Reports (British Series) 33, 309-326

Burl, A. 1987. *The Stonehenge People: Life and Death at the World's Greatest Stone Circle*. London: Guild Publishing

Burl, A. 1994. 'Stonehenge: slaughter, sacrifice and sunshine.' *Wiltshire Archaeological and Natural History Society Magazine* 87, 85-95

Burl, A. 2000. *The Stone Circles of Britain, Ireland and Brittany*. Yale: University Press

Case, H. 1995. 'Beakers: loosening a stereotype.' In I. Kinnes & G. Varndell (eds), *'Unbaked Urns of Rudely Shape': Essays on British and Irish Pottery*. Oxford: Oxbow Monograph 55, 55-68

Castledon, R. 1993. *The Making of Stonehenge*. London and New York: Routledge

Clark, J.G.D. 1936. 'The timber monument at Arminghall and its affinities.' *Proceedings of the Prehistoric Society* 2, 1-51.

Cleal, R. 1995a. 'The first monument, phase 1.' In R.M.J. Cleal *et al.*, *Stonehenge in its Landscape: Twentieth-century Excavations*. London: English Heritage Archaeological Report 10, chapter 5

Cleal, R. 1995b. 'A change of emphasis, phase 2.' In R.M.J. Cleal *et al.*, *Stonehenge in its Landscape: Twentieth-century Excavations*. London: English Heritage Archaeological Report 10, chapter 6

Cleal, R. 1995c. 'The stone settings, phase 3.' In R.M.J. Cleal *et al.*, *Stonehenge in its Landscape: Twentieth-century Excavations*. London: English Heritage Archaeological Report 10, chapter 7

Cleal, R. 1995d. 'Prehistoric pottery.' In R.M.J. Cleal *et al.*, *Stonehenge in its Landscape: Twentieth-century Excavations*. London: English Heritage Archaeological Report 10, 349-67

Cleal, R. & Allen, M.J. 1995a. 'Stonehenge in its landscape.' In R.M.J. Cleal *et al.*, *Stonehenge in its Landscape: Twentieth-century Excavations*. London: English Heritage Archaeological Report 10, chapter 10

Cleal, R. & Allen, M.J. 1995b. 'The visual envelope.' In R.M.J. Cleal *et al.*, *Stonehenge in its Landscape: Twentieth-century Excavations*. London: English Heritage Archaeological Report 10, 34-40

Cleal, R.M.J., Walker, K.E. & Montague, R. 1995. *Stonehenge in its Landscape: Twentieth-century Excavations*. London: English Heritage Archaeological Report

Coles, B. & Coles, J. 1986. *Sweet Track to Glastonbury: the Somerset Levels in Prehistory*. London: Thames and Hudson

Condit, T. & Simpson, D. 1998. 'Irish hengiform enclosures and related monuments: a review.' In A. Gibson & D. Simpson (eds), *Prehistoric Ritual and Religion*. Stroud: Sutton Publishing, 45-61

Cooney, G. 2000. *Landscapes of Neolithic Ireland*. London: Routledge

Darvill, T.C. 1996. 'Neolithic buildings in England, Wales and the Isle of Man.' In T.C. Darvill & J.S. Thomas (eds), *Neolithic Houses in Northwest Europe and Beyond*. Oxford: Oxbow (Neolithic Studies Group Seminar Papers 1), 77-112

Darvill, T.C. 1997. 'Ever increasing circles: the sacred geographies of Stonehenge and its landscape.' In B. Cunliffe & C. Renfrew (eds), *Science and Stonehenge*. Oxford and New York: Oxford University Press, 167-202

Dames, M. 1977. *The Avebury Cycle*. London: Thames and Hudson Ltd

Dymond, D.P. 1965. Grassington, W.R. (90). *Yorkshire Archaeological Journal* XLI (163), 323-4

Earle, T.K. 1991. 'Property rights and the evolution of chiefdoms.' In T.K. Earle (ed.), *Chiefdoms: Power, Economy and Ideology*. Cambridge: University Press, 71-99

Gibson, A. 1994. 'Excavations at the Sarn-y-bryn-caled cursus complex, Welshpool, Powys, and the timber circles of Great Britain and Ireland.' *Proceedings of the Prehistoric Society* 60, 143-224

Gibson, A. 1998. *Stonehenge and Timber Circles*. Stroud: Tempus

Gray, H.St.G. 1903. 'On the excavations at Arbor Low, 1901-1902.' *Archaeologia* 58 (2), 461-98

Gray, H.St.G. 1934. 'The Avebury excavations, 1908-1922.' *Archaeologia* 84, 99-162

Harding, A.F. 1981. 'Excavations in the prehistoric ritual complex near Milfield, Northumberland.' *Proceedings of the Prehistoric Society* 47, 87-135

Harding, A. 2000. 'Henge monuments and landscape features in northern England: monumentality and nature.' In A. Ritchie (ed.), *Neolithic Orkney in its European Context*. Cambridge: McDonald Institute Monographs, 267-75

Harding, A.F. & Lee, G.E. 1987. *Henge Monuments and Related Sites of Great Britain*. Oxford: British Archaeological Reports (British Series) 175

Harding, J. 2000. 'Later Neolithic Ceremonial Centres, Ritual and Pilgrimage: the Monument Complex of Thornborough, North Yorkshire.' In A. Ritchie (ed.), *Neolithic Orkney in its European Context*. Cambridge: McDonald Institute Monographs, 31–46

Hartwell, B. 1998. 'The Ballynahatty complex.' In A. Gibson & D. Simpson (eds), *Prehistoric Ritual and Religion*. Stroud: Sutton Publishing

Healy, F. 1997. 'Site 3. Flagstones.' In Smith, R.J.C. *et al.*, *Excavations Along the Route of the Dorchester By-pass, Dorset, 1986-8*. Salisbury: Wessex Archaeology Report No. 11, 27–48

Hodder, I. 1990. *The Domestication of Europe*. Oxford: Blackwell

Houlder, C. 1968. The henge monuments at Llandegai. *Antiquity* XLII (166), 216–21

Kinnes, I.A. 1979. *Round Barrows and Ring-ditches in the British Neolithic*. London: British Museum Occasional Paper 7

Kinnes, I., Gibson, A., Ambers, J., Bowman, S., Leese, M. & Boast, R. 1981. 'Radiocarbon dating and British Beakers: the British Museum Programme.' *Scottish Archaeological Review* 8, 35–68

Kinnes, I., Schadla-Hall, T., Chadwick, P., & Dean, P. 1983. 'Duggleby Howe Reconsidered.' *Archaeological Journal* 140, 83–108

McKinley, J.I. 1995. 'Human bone.' In R.M.J. Cleal *et al.*, *Stonehenge in its Landscape: Twentieth-century Excavations*. London: English Heritage Archaeological Report 10, 451–61

Meaden, T. 1997. *Stonehenge: the Secret of the Solstice*. London: Souvenir Press

Meaden, T. 1999. *The Secrets of the Avebury Stones: Britain's Greatest Megalithic Temple*. London: Souvenir Press

Mercer, R.J. 1981. 'The excavation of a late Neolithic Henge-type enclosure at Balfarg, Markinch, Fife, Scotland, 1977-78.' *Proceedings of the Society of Antiquaries of Scotland* 111, 63–171

McInnes, I.J. 1964. 'A class II henge in the East Riding of Yorkshire.' *Antiquity* 38, 218-9

Miket, R. 1985. 'Ritual enclosures at Whitton Hill, Northumberland.' *Proceedings of the Prehistoric Society* 51, 137–48

Montague, R. 1995a. 'Chalk objects.' In R.M.J. Cleal *et al.*, *Stonehenge in its Landscape: Twentieth-century Excavations*. London: English Heritage Archaeological Report 10, 399–407

Montague, R. 1995b. 'Bone and antler small objects.' In R.M.J. Cleal *et al.*, *Stonehenge in its Landscape: Twentieth-century Excavations*. London: English Heritage Archaeological Report 10, 407-14

Mortimer, J.R. 1905. *Forty Years' Researches in British and Saxon Burial Mounds of East Yorkshire*. London: A. Brown and Sons

Parker Pearson, M. & Ramilisonina. 1998. 'Stonehenge for the ancestors: the stones pass on the message.' *Antiquity* 72 (276), 308-26

Pitts, M. 2000. *Hengeworld*. London: Century

Pitts, M. & Whittle, A.W.R. 1992. 'The development and date of Avebury.' *Proceedings of the Prehistoric Society* 48, 203-26

Pollard, J. 1992. 'The Sanctuary, Overton Hill, Wiltshire: a reassessment.' *Proceedings of the Prehistoric Society* 58, 213-26

Pollard, J. 1995. 'Inscribing space: formal deposition at the later Neolithic monument of Woodhenge, Wiltshire.' *Proceedings of the Prehistoric Society* 61, 137-56

Pollard, J. & Ruggles, C. 2001. 'Shifting perceptions: spatial order, cosmology, and patterns of deposition at Stonehenge.' *Cambridge Archaeological Journal* 11 (1), 69-90

Pryor, F., French, C., Crowther, D., Gurney, D., Simpson, G. & Taylor, M. 1985. *The Fenland Project, No. 1: Archaeology and Environment in the Lower Welland Valley*. Cambridge: East Anglian Archaeology 27

RCHME. 1979. *Stonehenge and its Environs*. Edinburgh: HMSO

Renfrew, C. 1973. 'Monuments, mobilisation and social organisation in Neolithic Wessex.' In C. Renfrew (ed.) *The Explanation of Cultural Change*. London: Gerald Duckworth, 539-58

Renfrew, C. 1979. *Investigations in Orkney*. London: Society of Antiquaries of London Research Report XXXVIII

Richards, J. 1990. *The Stonehenge Environs Project*. London: English Heritage Archaeological Report No. 16

Richards, C. 1992. Barnhouse and Maeshowe. *Current Archaeology* 131, 444-7

Richards, C. 1996. 'Henges and water: towards an elemental understanding of monumentality and landscape in late Neolithic Britain.' *Journal of Material Culture* 1 (3), 313-36

Richards, C. & Thomas, J. 1984. 'Ritual activity and structured deposition in later Neolithic Wessex.' In R. Bradley & J. Gardiner (eds), *Neolithic Studies: A Review of Some Current Research*. Oxford: British Archaeological Reports (British Series) 133, 189-218

Ritchie, J.N.G. 1975-6. 'The Stones of Stenness, Orkney.' *Proceedings of the Society of Antiquaries of Scotland* 107, 1-60

Ruggles, C. 1996. 'Archaeoastronomy in Europe.' In. C. Walker (ed.), *Astronomy Before the Telescope*. London: British Museum Press, 15-27

Ruggles, C. 1997. 'Astronomy and Stonehenge.' In B. Cunliffe & C. Renfrew (eds), *Science and Stonehenge*. Oxford and New York: Oxford University Press, 203-30

Ruggles, C. 1999. *Astronomy in Prehistoric Britain and Ireland*. New Haven and London: Yale University Press

Saville, A. 1983. 'Excavations at Condicote henge monument, Gloucestershire, 1977.' *Transactions of the Bristol and Gloucestershire Archaeological Society* 101, 21-47

Serjeantson, D. & Gardiner, J. 1995. 'Red deer implements and ox scapula shovels.' In R.M.J. Cleal *et al.*, *Stonehenge in its Landscape: Twentieth-century Excavations*. London: English Heritage Archaeological Report 10, 414-30

Sherratt, A. 1997. 'Cups that cheered: the introduction of alcohol to prehistoric Europe.' Reprinted in A. Sherratt, *Economy and Society in Prehistoric Europe. Changing Perspectives*. Edinburgh: University Press, 376-402

Smith, I.F. 1965. *Windmill Hill and Avebury*. Oxford: Clarendon Press

Smith, R.J.C., Healy, F., Allen, M.J., Morris, E.L., Barnes, I. & Woodward, P.J. 1997. *Excavations Along the Route of the Dorchester By-pass, Dorset, 1986-8*. Salisbury: Wessex Archaeology Report No. 11

Startin, W. & Bradley, R.J. 1981. 'Some notes on work organisation and society in prehistoric Wessex.' In C. Ruggles & A.W.R. Whittle (eds) *Astronomy and Society during the Period 4000-1500 BC*. Oxford: British Archaeological Reports (British Series) 88, 289-96

Shennan, S. 1982. 'Ideology, change and the European Bronze Age.' In I. Hodder (ed.) *Symbolic and Structural Archaeology*. Cambridge: University Press, 155-61

Stoertz, C. 1997. *Ancient Landscapes of the Yorkshire Wolds: Aerial Photographic Transcriptions and Analysis*. Swindon: Royal Commission on the Historical Monuments of England.

Thomas, J. 1996. *Time, Culture and Identity: an Interpretive Archaeology*. London and New York: Routledge

Thomas, J. 1999. *Understanding the Neolithic*. London and New York: Routledge

Thomas, N. 1955. 'The Thornborough Circles, near Ripon, North Riding.' *Yorkshire Archaeological Journal* 38, 425-45

Thorpe, I. & Richards, C. 1984. 'The decline of ritual authority and the introduction of Beakers into Britain.' In R. Bradley & J. Gardiner (eds), *Neolithic Studies. A Review of Some Current Research*. Oxford: British Archaeological Reports (British Series) 133, 67- 84

Topping, P. 1992. 'The Penrith henges: a survey by the Royal Commission on the Historical Monuments of England.' *Proceedings of the Prehistoric Society* 58, 249-64

Vatcher, F. 1960. 'Thornborough cursus, Yorks.' *Yorkshire Archaeological Journal* 40 (158), 169-82

Waddington, C. 1996. 'Putting rock art to use. A model of early Neolithic transhumance in north Northumberland.' In P. Frodsham (ed.), 'Neolithic Studies in No-Man's Land. Papers on the Neolithic of Northern England from the Trent to the Tweed.' *Northern Archaeology* 13/14 (Special Edition), 147-78

Wainwright, G.J. 1971. 'The excavation of a late Neolithic enclosure at Marden, Wiltshire.' *Antiquaries Journal* 51, 177-236

Wainwright, G.J. 1979. *Mount Pleasant, Dorset: Excavations 1970-1971*. London: Society of Antiquaries (Report of the Research Committee No XXXVII)

Wainwright, G.J. 1989. *The Henge Monuments: Ceremony and Society in Prehistoric Britain*. London: Thames and Hudson

Wainwright, G.J. & Longworth, I.H. 1971. *Durrington Walls: Excavations 1966-1968*. London: Society of Antiquaries (Report of the Research Committee No. XXIX)

Watson, A. 2001. 'Composing Avebury.' *World Archaeology* 33 (2), 296-314

Whittle, A. 1997. 'Remembered and imagined belongings: Stonehenge in its traditions and structures of meaning.' In B. Cunliffe & C. Renfrew (eds), *Science and Stonehenge*. Oxford and New York: Oxford University Press, 145-66

Whittle, A., Atkinson, R.J.C., Chambers, R. & Thomas, N. 1992. 'Excavations in the Neolithic and Bronze Age complex at Dorchester on Thames, Oxfordshire, 1947-1952 and 1981.' *Proceedings of the Prehistoric Society* 58, 143-202

Whittle, A., Pollard, J. & Grigson, C. 1999. *The Harmony of Symbols. The Windmill Hill Causewayed Enclosure, Wiltshire*. Oxford: Oxbow Books

Woodward, A. 2000. *British Barrows. A Matter of Life and Death*. Stroud: Tempus

INDEX

References in **bold** denote page numbers of illustrations

Akeld, Northumberland **43**
alcohol 118
Aldwincle 1, Northamptonshire **19**
ancestry 9, 23-6, 29, 31, 54, 113-5
animal bone 13, 34, 40, 46, 67, 68, **77**, 80, 81
antler 46, 67-8, **68**
Arbor Low, Derbyshire **10**, 65, 66, 67, 71, 73
Arminghall, Norfolk 32, **32**, 72, 73
astronomy 9, 45-8, **46**
   see also moon, sky, solstices
Avebury, Wiltshire 6, **11**, 12, **14**, 15, 32, 38, 39, 48-50, **49**, **50**, 55, 60, 63, 64, 69, 71, **73**, 76, 78, 84, 86, **86**, 114-6, **colour plates 2, 5-10**
   see also Beckhampton Avenue, West Kennet Avenue

Balfarg Riding School, Fife 12, **14**, 15, **16**, 17, 19, 65
Barrow Hills, Oxfordshire **28**
Beaker pottery 31, 110, **111**, 112, 114, 117, 118
   and related grave-goods 110, **111**, 117, 119
Beckhampton Avenue, Avebury, Wiltshire 49, **49**, 63
bone objects **68**
Boynton 3, East Yorkshire **19**
Bradley, Richard 88, 90

Bull Ring, Derbyshire 55
Burl, Aubrey 106

Cairnpapple Hill, Lothian 55
Cana Barn, North Yorkshire **87**, **91**, 92, 97, **99**, 100
Carn Brae, Cornwall 26
carved chalk 46, 52, **52**, 67, 68, **68**, **77**, 81
Castle Dykes, North Yorkshire **87**, 100, 101, **102**
Catterick, North Yorkshire 100
chiefdoms 84-6, 88, 106
chronology *see* radiocarbon dates
circles and circularity 36, 38, 39, 43, 44, 48, 51, 54, 56, 78, 80
   see also spirals
City Farm 4, Oxfordshire **20**
classic henges 6, 12, 13, 20-2, 26, 27, 29, 33, 34, 36, 92
Cleal, Ros 13
Condicote, Gloucestershire **14**, 15, 31, **31**, **37**, 38
Coneybury Hill, Wiltshire 12, **14**, 15, **16**, 20-2, **23**, 26, 29, 45, 46, 51
Coupland, Northumberland 42, **43**
coves 71, 78, 119
cremations 19, 20, 27, 28, 46, 65, 67, 113, 114, 116
Crickley Hill, Gloucestershire 26
cup-and-ring marks 56, **57**

cursuses *see* Dorchester on Thames cursus, Maxey cursus, Thornborough cursus

Dames, Michael 48-51
Darvill, Tim 45, 46, 81
Devil's Arrows, North Yorkshire **91**, 97, 98
Devil's Quoits, Oxfordshire **14**, 15, 30, **31**, 36, **37**, 38, 65, 67, 71, 74, 107, 108, 116, 119, **120**, 121
Dorchester, Dorset 13, 21, **24**; timber circle 22, **24**
Dorchester on Thames, Oxfordshire 30, 84, 89, **89**, 96
   Big Rings 28, 30, 31, 89, 96
   cursus 89, **89**, 96
   Site IV-VI, 28, **29**, 36, **37**, 96, 113; Site 2, 12, **14**, 15, **16**, 28, **29**, 36, **37**
Duggleby Howe, East Yorkshire 17, **21**, 101, **114**, 116
Durrington Walls, Wiltshire **11**, **14**, 15, 21, 22, **23**, 33, 38, 40, 46, 52, 60, 61, **61**, 63, 74, 75, **75**, 78, 80, 84, 86, **86**, 115, 116

early Bronze Age 108, 121
   round barrows and cemeteries **77**, 119, **120**, 121
   single-grave burials 108, **108**, 109, 110, 112, 119
   see also Beakers and related grave-goods

early Neolithic 9, 23
  human bone 9, 24, **26**, 113
  causewayed enclosure **8**, 9,
    13, 17, 26, **27**, 38
  chambered tombs **8**-9, 24-6,
    26
  long barrows 9, 24, **28**, 112,
    113
East Anglia 84, 112
England, midlands 84, 112;
  north-east 112
  see also East Anglia, Lake
    District, Peak District,
    Thames Valley, Wessex
    chalkland, Yorkshire
Ewart, Northumberland **43**

feasting 34, 80, 118
Ferrybridge, South Yorkshire
  87, 100
fertility 49-54, 68, 74, 78
fieldwalking 60-2, **62**
Firtree Farm, Dorset **20**
Flagstones, Dorset 13, **16**, 21,
  24, 28, 92
flint 46, 60-2, 67, 68, **77**, 80,
  81, 98
formative henges 13, 17, 19,
  20, 26, 27, 32, 34, 36, 45,
  54, 92, 113

Gibson, Alex 32, 75
God-dolly, Somerset Levels
  52, 53, **53**
Gorsey Bigbury, Somerset **14**,
  15, 38, 65, 67, 117
Great Langdale 97
Grindale 1, East Yorkshire **19**
Grooved Ware **8**, 9, 12, 34,
  58, 67, **77**, 80, 118

Hambledon Hill, Dorset **27**
Handley 26 and 27, Dorset **19**
Harding, Anthony 42
henge enclosures 6, **11**,
  31, 38, 60, 63, 64, 66,
  83, 87
hengiforms 83
Hodder, Ian 40, 41
Holborough, Kent **19**
houses **55**, 56

human bone 13, 27, 28, 31,
  32, 41, 46, 56, 67, 68, **68**,
  71, **77**, 81, 113-5, 117
  see also cremations
Hutton Moor, North
  Yorkshire **87**, **91**, 92, 97,
  99, 100

Ireland 17, 19, 55, 56, 106
  art 56, **57**
  Ballynahatty, Co. Down 19,
    106
  River Boyne 17, 19
  Tara, Co. Meath 19
  see also passage graves

King Arthur's Round Table,
  Cumbria 65, 88, **104**, 105
Knowlton, Dorset **86**

labour estimates 86-8, 109
Lake District 97, 105, 106
Lincolnshire Wolds 100
lithics *see* flint
Little Round Table, Cumbria
  105
Litton Cheney 1, Dorset **20**
Llandegai A, Gwynedd 12,
  14, 15, **16**, 17, 19, 27, 37,
  37, 113
Long Meg, Cumbria 58, **58**

Maes Howe, Orkney 17, 19,
  20
Maiden's Grave, Rudston, East
  Yorkshire **87**, 101, 102,
  103
Marden, Wiltshire **11**, **14**, 15,
  31, 38, 54, 55, 66, 84, **86**
Maumbury Rings, Dorset **14**,
  15, 21, **24**, **25**, 30, **37**, **38**,
  39, 40, 52, 53, 115
Maxey, Cambridgeshire 89,
  89, 96, 97
  henge 89, **89**, 96
  cursus 89, **89**, 96
Mayburgh, Cumbria 64, **64**,
  65, **70**, 88, **104**, 106
Meaden, Terrence 48, 50, 51
Milfield Basin,
  Northumberland 42, **43**

Milfield North **14**, 15, **37**,
  38, 42, **43**, 54, 55, 67, 70,
  72, **72**
Milfield North reconstruction
  colour plate 11
Milfield South **43**, 54, 55,
  70, **72**
  see also Akeld, Coupland,
    Ewart, Yeavering
mini-henges 6, **29**, 83, 84, 87,
  96, 113
Mother Goddess 48-52
moon 45, 47, 48, 51, 71
Mount Pleasant, Dorset **11**, **14**,
  15, 22, **24**, 30, 31, 38, 40,
  52, **52**, 66, 74, 75, **76**, 78,
  80, 81, 84, 115, **118**, 119
Morwick Mill,
  Northumberland **57**, 58

Neolithic round barrows and
  ring ditches 13, **16**, 17, **19**,
  24, 112-4, **114**, 116, 119
Newnham Murren,
  Oxfordshire **20**
Newton Kyme, North
  Yorkshire **87**, **99**, 100
North Mains, Perth and
  Kinross 32, **32**, 72, 73
Nunwick, North Yorkshire
  87, **91**, 92, 97, **99**

Orkney 12, 13, 19-21, 34, 41,
  41, 42, 56, 73, 74

passage graves 17, 56
Peak District 56, 112
Pennines *see* Yorkshire Dales
pilgrimage and pilgrims 98,
  100, 105, 106
pit circles 72, **72**, 73, 97, 113;
  pits 70, 72
polished stone axes *see* stone
  axes
Pollard, Josh 46-7, 78, 80
posts *see* timber posts
pottery 41, 80, 81
  see also Grooved Ware,
    Beakers
prestige goods economy 109-
  12, 116, 117

radiocarbon dates 11-3, **14**, 15, 33, 53, 84, 107, 108, 111, 117, 119
Raunds, Northamptonshire **108, 111**
Renfrew, Colin 84-7, 105
Richards, Colin 41-3, 51
Ring of Brodgar, Orkney 12, 41, 42, **41, 42**, 54, 73, **4**
ritual authority structure 109, 110, 112, 116, 117
rivers 56
    River Eamont 64
    River Swale 98
    River Ure 87, 90, **91**, 97-100, **101**
    River Wharfe 100
    see also water
Ruggles, Clive 46, 47

Salisbury Plain, Wiltshire 13, 20, **23**, 29, 45, **48**, 115, **120**
Sanctuary, Wiltshire 115
Sarn-y-Bryn-Caled Site 2, Powys 20
Scotland, central 112
Shetland 56
sky 44, 45, 47, 48, 51, 52, 82
solstices 45-7, 50, 51, 81
spirals **57**, 58, **58**
Stanton Harcourt, Oxfordshire 116, 119, **120**, 121
standing stones 45, **47**, 50, 51, 65, **66**, 70-2, **73**, 76, **76**, 78, **79**, 119
stone axes 56, 97, **97**, 99, 100

stone circles 45, **46**, **47**, 48-51, 71, 73-6, **74**, 78, **79**, **colour plates 1, 2, 5-10, 12 & 13**
Stonehenge, Wiltshire 6, 12, 13, **14**, 15, **16**, 17, 20, 21, **23**, 27-9, 32, 34, 36, **37**, 38, 45, 46, **46**, **47**, 51-3, 65, **66**, 67, **68**, 73, 75, 76, **79**, 81, 113, 115, 117-9, 121, **colour plates 1, 12 & 13**
Stones of Stenness, Orkney 12, 13, **14**, **16**, 17, 22, 26, **37**, 41, **41**, 42, 54, 72, 74, **74**, **colour plate 3**

Thames Valley 30, 31, **31**, 74, 84, 112, 116, 119
Thomas, Julian 112
Thornborough, North Yorkshire 61, 62, **62**, 64, 69, **87**, 90, **91**, 92, 95-9, 105, 106, **15**
    cursus 85, **91**, 92, 93
    central henge **40, 65, 70, 85, 91**, 92-4, **94, 99**
    northern henge **91, 99**
    southern henge **14**, 15, **91**, 93-5, **93, 95, 96, 99**, 107, 108
timber circles 32, 33, 45, 72-5, **75-7**, 78, 80, 81, 115; timber posts 65, **66**, 70-2, **colour plate 11**
Trent Valley 100

volcanic eruption 53, 54

water 54-6
Wensleydale 97, 100
Wessex chalkland **11**, 40, 52, 64, 74, 75, 84-6, **86**, 88, 115
West Kennet Avenue, Avebury, Wiltshire 48, 49, **49**, 63, 87, 117, **5**
palisade enclosures 115
tomb **8, 26**
Westwell, Gloucestershire **31**
Whitegrounds, East Yorkshire **16**
Whitton Hill 1, Northumberland 12, **37**
Windmill Hill, Wiltshire **8**
Wold Newton 284, East Yorkshire 102
Woodhenge, Wiltshire **14**, 15, 21-2, **23**, 33, **33**, 36, **37**, 38, 40, 45, 46, 51, 60-1, **61**, 74, **77**, 78, 80, 81, 115, 117, **colour plate 14**
Woodlands pit group 61, **61**
Wyke Down, Dorset **14**, 15, 28, **30**, 36, **37**, 38, 67, 113

Yarnbury, North Yorkshire **87**, 100
Yeavering, Northumberland **43, 44**
Yorkshire 84, 87, 88, **87**, 90, 103, 104
    East Riding 101-3, 112, 116
    Dales 88, 100, 101
    Wolds 88, 97, 102, 112